"Teenagers Living In A Culture Of Darkness

Living Together… All Alone."

Love's The Only House

Martina McBride

Disclaimer

This Book, like Life itself, offers no guarantees, expressed or implied.

Raise Kids At Your Own Risk.

Copyright

Dedicated

To My Grandchildren

(In Reverse Order Of Appearance)

Penelope – The Athlete

Louis – The Patriot

Emily – The Scientist

Will – The Knight Errant

Cate – The Missionary

Luke – The Cool Hand

And

To Their Mothers

Who Taught Me All I Know!

And

To Their Mother

Who Took The Journey With Me

Table of Contents

FORWARD

Hello, I am Bill Oliver.

For forty years now, I have been fighting to save kids from America's (World's) Toxic Culture. This book contains lessons learned along the way. I did not do many of these as I raised my two girls. I didn't know about them. They are what I should have done. Shoulda, coulda, woulda.

I became involved with kids and The Toxic Culture because my older daughter ran away from home when she was fifteen years old. This was in 1978... before the War on Drugs... before Nancy Reagen... before DARE... before Red Ribbon Week... before anything. My generation of parents learned about America's Toxic Culture the hard way. Not from books we read but from lives we led.

I made a promise. If I ever get her back, I will devote the rest of my life helping parents prevent what had happened to us.

One thing led to another and I became an "expert". That is easy to do when nobody knows anything about an issue. I developed a training program for parents called Parent To Parent. It was taught to parents by parents. It reached over three million parents.

I was taught in a Leadership Course that there are three reasons people have difficulty in any job:

> They don't know <u>what</u> the job is.

> They don't know <u>how</u> to do the job.

> Something or someone <u>interferes</u> with their desire or ability to do the job.

As a result, I want you to have some idea:

> What The Job Is.

> How To Do The Job.

> How To Combat ... America's Toxic Culture.

Let's get the first thing done... the job description...

As I see it, the parent's job is to **produce a dependable, responsible, functioning adult**. That's the goal... the vision... a mentally healthy, physically healthy, spiritually healthy adult.

You do not to raise a child... You want to raise an adult!

Now to the hard part...

Chapter One

THE YELLOW BRICK ROAD

One day, I was having lunch with a good friend who is a Child Psychologist when he turned to me and said, "Have you ever considered that raising kids is like Dorothy and the Wizard of OZ?"

I had to admit I had not... but then who had? Only my friend, Doctor Herb. He went on.

"Dorothy lived in Kansas." he said. "Kansas is a very orderly State. The crops grow in rows and the roads intersect at right angles. She lives there with Auntie Em, Uncle Something-or-other, three farmhands, and her dog, Toto. Even the movie shows Kansas in black and white."

"One day, a tornado sweeps Dorothy up and deposits her in a strange land full of Munchkins, Witches, and Yellow Brick Roads... not to mention a very dead witch upon whom her house had fallen. Seeing this, Dorothy speaks that classic line, 'Toto, we're not in Kansas anymore."

Herb goes on.

"Dorothy is told that only the Great and Powerful Wizard of Oz can help her get back to Kansas. The Wizard lives in the Emerald City and all she has to do is follow the yellow brick road."

Herb goes on a roll.

"She and Toto set off to find the Wizard. Along way, she picks up three friends a Scarecrow with no brain, a Tin Woodsmen with no heart, and a Lion with no courage. They volunteer go with her to the Emerald City. It's like picking up Curly, Larry and Moe as companions."

"As they travel, they go through poppy fields that put them to sleep (Drugs?), they encounter trees that talk and flying monkeys... not to mention a very evil green witch who is allergic to water."

"To make a long story short, they eventually get to meet the Wizard, the all-powerful, great Oz. There is smoke. There's fire. There's lights and a face on the wall."

"The little dog, Toto, pulls aside a curtain and only to reveal a little man pulling rows of levers and shouting into a microphone."

"The Wizard Of Oz was a fake, said Herb."

"However, in their struggles, the Scarecrow developed a brain... Wisdom. The Tin Woodsman... a heart... Love. The Cowardly Lion now had Courage. Once she realizes that development, she clicks the ruby slippers three times and, suddenly, is back in Kansas."

My purpose in writing this book is to help you navigate the strange land of Adolescence to get back to Kansas... Sanity.

If you are ready, we can now set off down the Yellow Brick Road... in search of Wisdom, Love, and Courage. Let's roll!

ARE YOU ANYBODY... ?

I was in Washington to make a presentation to some members of the U.S. House of Representatives because they were concerned about the American drug policy. The only available flight from Atlanta to D.C. put me at National Airport three hours before I was to speak; so, I had some time to kill.

I had been to the Washington Monument. I had done the Smithsonian and the other major buildings. I decided to the Capitol Building to see the House and Senate Chambers. After all, the Capitol was near where I was to speak, and it had been years since I had been there.

Apparently, half the fifth and sixth grade teachers in the U.S. had chosen that fine spring day for their students to make the same pilgrimage. The excited youngsters were so noisy, I decided, after about ten minutes of looking around, to just go outside and enjoy the spring air.

On my way out, I spotted a bank of phones and headed towards them to call my office. (This was BC... before Cells). While I was dialing the number, I felt a tug at about pocket-level of my coat. I looked down, and there was what looked to be a little fifth grade boy and his buddy. "Yes," I said. "Can I help you?"

The youngster doing the tugging said, "Excuse me, but are you a senator?" I guess he thought that because I was the only person in the immediate vicinity wearing a pin-striped suit, wingtip shoes, and a tie.

"No, I'm not a senator."

Are you a member of the House of Representatives?"

"No, I'm not a member of the House."

"Then you must be a cabinet secretary." One thing was certain: he knew his chain of command perfectly and had obviously done well in his civics class.

"No," I said, becoming a bit irritated. "I'm not a cabinet secretary."

And then the boy asked a question I was not prepared to hear. "Well, are you anybody important at all?"

The question so surprised me that I answered it by saying, "No, I'm not anybody important at all," at which point he and his buddy headed down the hall. As the boys departed, the one with all the questions called over his shoulder, saying, "If you ever want to be, we'll vote for you."

After finishing my call and moving outside, I began thinking about what the boy had asked: Was I anybody important, at all? I decided that, if ever asked that question again, I would give a very different answer because I did not like having to admit that I was not important. And, after thinking about it, I realized the answer I gave the boys was not correct.

While I am not important in the sense that those youngsters thought of importance, I am important in a different way. I am important in the lives of a handful of people. In fact, in those people's lives, I am more than important, much more. I am primary.

To my wife, I am more important than all the congressmen who have ever been, all the senators who ever sat, and all the cabinet secretaries ever appointed.

To my daughters, I am more important than all of the above put together.

To my grandchildren, who are not yet old enough to even know the President's name, I am a most important guy; I am their "Pop Pop, Entertainer, Gift Giver, and All-around Good Guy"

Yes, I am a primary person in the lives of a handful of people. To them, I am more than important; I am primary.

That fact made me realize that, in our role as parents, all of us are primary in somebody's life. We may not be politically important. We may not be famous. But, in the lives of our children, we are a primary person for better or worse. Like it or not, mom or dad, you are the primary person in your child's life. It is to you your child looks for guidance, for teaching, for discipline, for love, for protection, and for caring. Only you can provide these precious things in the quantity and quality that a child deserves and a parent can best deliver. Surely programs in school can help, but you are more important than they are. You are more important than important; you are primary. Without you, all other programs fail.

There are three reasons you are so primary in your child's life. He first is simply time on task.

Time On Task

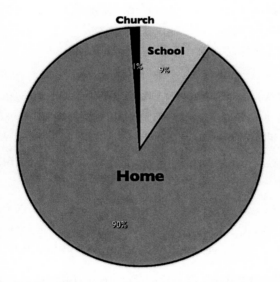

Take a child's life from zero to, say, eighteen years of age and then shrink those eighteen years down to sixty minutes. Then ask yourself this question: of those sixty minutes, how many minutes is the child in school? It turns out to be about 5.6 minutes; less than ten percent of that child's youth will be spend in school.

For example, the school year is only 180 days long. The school day is only about six hours. Most children do not start school until they are four or five years of age. School does not open on the weekend, and it is traditionally closed for the summer. If you just do the math, each child is in school about 5.6 minutes of the time on that sixty minute clock face.

If your child is heavily involved with church, synagogue, mosque, or other value-oriented institutions, on that same clock face, the time spent in the environment of organized religion is about .7 minutes. So, less than one-sixtieth of that time from zero to eighteen will be involved with church, synagogue, or mosque.

The rest of the time, fully 90 percent of the child's life from zero to eighteen is in the hands of the family. And when I say family, I mean in your hands. So, just by the simple fact of time, you are primary in your child's life.

Knowledge

Second, you are primary in your child's life because of **your knowledge** of him as a person. You have been with your child since the day of birth. You have an intuition, a feeling, about her that has grown from the day you took that baby out of the hospital until today. No professional can have that sense of feeling or intuition because, unlike you, they have not been with your child during the development years.

Influence

And third, you are primary in your child's life because of **your influence**. Study after study says that what parents say and what parents talk about with their children are primary influences in a young people's decision to use or not use drugs. The same holds true in their decision to be violent or not to be violent. And, their decision to be sexually active or not sexually active.

The great mistake most of us make is believing, if we get a child into the right school and into the right neighborhood and into the right program, we have done our job as a father or mother. No. Nothing could be further from the truth. That might make you a Placement Service. It does not make you a mother or father.

No Fluffed-up Chicken

Before asking you to read further, there is something I think you should know about this book, something that is summed up in a story frequently told in Gainesville, Georgia. At one time, that town was the Chicken Capital of the World, and this story is about a Gainesville resident who was widely recognized as the world's greatest chicken salesman. One Saturday afternoon, so the story goes, the terrific salesman was down to his last chicken. A lady came into his store and said, "Sir, may I see a chicken?"

The salesman reached under the counter and pulled up his last chicken. The lady said, "Oh, that's a nice chicken." He agreed and said it would cost her three dollars. "May I see another?" she asked.

He put the chicken back under the counter, fluffed up its feathers and placed it back on the counter. She said, "Oh, that's a nice chicken, too."

"Yes, ma'am, it's bigger than the other one; so, I'm asking $3.50 for it."

Whereupon the lady said, "I'll take both of them."

I repeat this story because I want this book to avoid being a fluffed up chicken. I want it to be the real thing... something realistic... something meaningful.

CHAPTER TWO

THE TOXIC CULTURE

Love Canal

In the 1960's, Love Canal, a residential development in the state of New York, became the focus of national attention. It was an attractive community, the sort you might imagine being a perfect place to raise children. But, when many of the youngsters living at Love Canal became ill, tests revealed they had cancer, and the death rate soared. To a lesser degree, the adults were also affected. It was eventually discovered that the community had been built on the site of a toxic chemical waste dump, which was bit by bit, day by day, destroying the bodies of the inhabitants, especially the children. The community became so permeated by toxins that the residents had to move in order to save their lives.

Today, we are experiencing something similar. More and more American families are discovering the alarming truth: their communities have become a waste dump, a sewer, for the Toxic Culture, and their children are playing in it. Therefore, the pollutants that continually flow into that dump are bit by bit, day by day, mentally and physically destroying highly susceptible children and, to a lesser degree, affecting the more resistant adults.

Things have, indeed, changed in America. Today's parents face a set of problems that is different from the set faced by previous generations. The set you face is different because the drug culture of the 1970's and early 80's, which promoted drug and alcohol use by children has experienced a potent negative synergism.

Think of drug and alcohol use by children as a toxic flow that seeps into a pool within your neighborhood. Chemicals like Crack, Meth, Pot, Ethyl Alcohol, Glue, Paint Thinner, and the so-called Energy Drinks flow copiously into our communities.

If that were not bad enough, that toxic flow is now merging with two additional toxic flows. The second is premature promiscuous sex by children.

The third is violence by children. All three, in my mind, flow together to form a toxic waste dump that masquerades as entertainment for children... as FUN. In and of themselves, each of these flows is dangerous; in combination, they are lethal.

Promiscuous sex, drugs, alcohol, and violence have always been around in some form, and they have been used to varying degrees by a limited number of adults as entertainment.

However, until very recently, they were never considered a child's pastime, a game for children to play. That is the terrifying phenomenon we must acknowledge. Furthermore, we must acknowledge that the Toxic Culture created by the blending of drugs, promiscuous sex, and violence has nick-named itself "Fun". And, Fun wants your child to come out and play.

Here is a partial list of Fruit produced by the Toxic Culture:

School Shootings

Teen Pregnancy

Bullying

School Dropout/Drop-in

Vandalism

Sexually Transmitted Disease

Addiction

Premature Deaths

Runaway

Gangs

Metal Detectors

Amotivational Syndrome

To just name a few!

(Note: You might wonder just what is "Amotivational Syndrome". That is a person who, like Rhett Butler talking to Scarlett O'Hara in Gone With The Wind, "Just Doesn't Give A Damn!")

This Toxic Culture that continually flows into the midst of our lives is very appealing to the young. So is that new kid on the block: the Internet. While there are scores of wondrous things about the Internet and we will not relinquish its ability to share information on a global basis, its technology has transformed our society and our relationships at such a startling speed, we have failed to notice certain of its effects.

Perhaps this example makes my point.

Lee Harvey Oswald, the man who assassinated John F. Kennedy, was said to be "a loner." As a result of the Internet, there are no more loners. Today's "loners" are wired. Today, no matter how twisted a mind may be, its owner can contact like minds and susceptible minds with a few key strokes on a computer.

Your child can get in touch with anybody in the world he or she wishes to contact via your home computer or the computers at their school and the local library. A lot of those Internet chat room pals and "on-line Gamers" they can meet are heavily involved in the sex, drugs, and violence dimension of America's Toxic Culture.

I loved the movie Amadeus. It is the story of Wolfgang Amadeus Mozart, the great Austrian composer.

In the movie, Mozart is asked by his apprentice, "How do you think your music affects people?"

Mozart answers, "When I play a Waltz, they dance. When I play a March, they go to war. When I play a Mass, they pray. Music puts you in touch with the mind of the composer."

Think what risk unrestricted Internet brings to the table... puts them in touch with the mind... of anybody... of everybody! The Internet doesn't create garbage... it simply spreads it.

When I refer to our Toxic Culture, I use the word "toxic" with great care. The culture that stalks your child is toxic, but it is not poisonous. A poisonous substance generally kills quickly; however, a toxic substance takes time to destroy. Its effects are cumulative. They build and build, over time, eventually constituting a lethal dose. The good news — if there is any about toxins — is their effects are, if caught in time, reversible. So, there is genuine hope for the child who has become charmed by any of the three flows that fill the pool of the Toxic Culture.

If, by now, you are beginning to feel that I may be some loony out to save America, let me assure you that saving America is not my goal. That task is far beyond my capabilities; however, I am eager to help you save your child from America's Toxic Culture. That is a task that is achievable; that is a task neither you nor I can ignore. We may not be able to eradicate the Toxic Culture's presence from our country, our town, our neighborhood, and our lives; nonetheless, you, as a parent, can take measures to insulate your child until he or she can safely make the passage from adolescence into adulthood.

Times Change… People Change

In this book, I use few statistics in my attempt to make my points because statistics, in all our minds, are about somebody else. (Some wag once said that 54% of all statistics are made up on the spot.)

Perhaps I can show you how rapidly we have changed and how accepting we are of the changes with a simple illustration. Every boy in my third grade class carried a Boy Scout knife. It was an integral part of Scouting, and we carried those knives to school. No one thought of those knives as weapons; they were tools used to carve wood, to create totem poles, to make model ships. But, today, if your child carries the basic tool of Scouting into the school building, your child will be suspended or expelled.

What has changed? Has the knife changed? No, it is the same knife that it has always been. So, exactly what has changed?

Have kids changed? Have we suddenly raised a generation of natural-born killers? What has happened?

I grew up in the 1950's. In the course of fifty years, we have gone from a time when a Scout knife was regarded as a useful tool, a badge of honor, to being regarded as a lethal weapon. We have gone from a time when schools were considered safe harbors for our youngsters to places where there are metal detectors at the door, a policeman on duty, and drug-sniffing dogs roaming the halls. In light of Columbine, Virginia Tech, and Sandy Hook, we are now considering arming the teachers. What has happened, and how did we get here?

When I was a child, I thought my mother possessed two of the attributes of God; I thought she was omnipotent and omnipresent. In actuality, the parents of that day were simply networking. A neighbor would not hesitate to say to my parents, a friend, or another member of the community, "I saw Billy do something."

Today, the kids are networking, but the parents are not. We have little idea of what takes place out of our line of vision.

The Sexual Revolution

I believe the metamorphisms of America's thought and action patterns were launched in the late 1950's when we began redefining "fun." In my mind, it started with the introduction of the magazine Playboy. Its publisher, Hugh Hefner, introduced what he dubbed "The Playboy Philosophy." The ideas and attitudes his philosophy served up were, for their time, earthshaking: sex is fun; therefore, sex should be regarded as entertainment. That was his creed.

We started talking around our kids about subjects that had never before been openly aired. It is already difficult to recall how different things were back then. For example — and I know how Victorian this will sound — my mother would not say the word "pregnant." She said, "PG." She would not even use the word. And, I am certain she never uttered the word "condom." While I am not going to argue whether her attitudes were good or bad, I do hold that, as a result of Hefner's magazine and his writings, the American population, as a whole, developed a new vocabulary and redefined sex as fun, as entertainment, as sport.

Of course, there is a pleasurable element to sex and always has been. There is no doubt about that. It was designed to be a consummation of a relationship, a relationship that is physical, mental, and spiritual. But, casual entertainment? No. It was never designed as entertainment. In slight defense of Hefner I add that, while he did see sex as entertainment for adults, I don't think he never, ever thought of it as an appropriate pastime for children. But, that is what it has become. Today, you are more likely to find his philosophy in action among middle school children than among the people gathered at a bar.

When the sex-as-fun philosophy was presented and embraced, it brought with it the element of death in the form of a host of diseases that we had never recognized, never heard of, and never considered part of a child's experiences. But, death is hiding in the shadows when children are drawn to the concept of promiscuous premature sex as entertainment. As a result, we now have syphilis, AIDS, and HPV and at the middle school and high school level and group orgies that spread these and other sexually transmitted diseases at alarming rates.

You know this is not a gross exaggeration if you have reviewed any of the statistics or perhaps watched a disturbing Frontline documentary about an outbreak of syphilis among children thirteen to seventeen in the Rockdale County area outside of

Atlanta. Documentation and treatment of seventeen cases of syphilis uncovered suburban afternoon sex marathons in which over 200 participants had experienced intercourse with from 100 to 200 partners each. A favorite "game" was to watch the Playboy Channel on cable and recreate, as a spectator sport, the activities portrayed. Sad to say, Rockdale is not an isolated example. Such activity stays underground until a communicable and trackable event surfaces.

The Chemical Revolution

A second revolution occurred at the beginning of the 1960's: the chemical revolution. It is the second toxic stream that feeds your community's toxic waste dump. In the 60's, we defined drugs and drunkenness as fun and initiated the "party till you puke" philosophy now embraced by kids. The first time we measured drug use by American kids was in the late 1970's. When we asked the teenagers of that day, "How many of you have used an illicit drug?" 40 percent of our children raised their hands, saying: "Yes, I have."

That shocked us and still should because the drug epidemic is the engine that drives a lot of the behavior that you read about in the paper. While drug use by children is no longer news and is seldom reported, the media does still take notice of some of the behavior that is caused as a result of drug use by children. Over the course of the next few chapters, I will say a great deal about drugs and their role in the Toxic Culture. At this point, however, I need to clearly introduce the concept of death: death as a result of overdose, mental death through addiction, and the spiritual death that results.

When I say "spiritual," I do not use the word in the religious sense. If you ever go into a drug treatment program or an alcohol treatment program, you will hear someone say, "This is a spiritual program." What they are saying and what I am saying is, in order to deal with the problem of drug or alcohol addiction, you have to work on the person from the inside out. You have to start with their heart in order to have a fighting chance of breaking the connection with your child and his or her need for that next fix. I assure you that when your child gravitates toward drugs and alcohol in their quest for fun and entertainment, death prepares

The Entertainment Revolution

We have labeled two of the toxic flows that fill the Toxic Culture's waste dump: the sexual revolution and the chemical revolution, which both share the same destination: death. The third flow is violence, which most certainly chooses death as its destination. We need to ask ourselves why is it that kids are going into their schools and killing people? I will tell you why: we have taught them to do it.

Violence and ensuing death are held up to our children as entertainment, as fun. Our children see slasher movies and begin to think it is funny and thrilling to watch people die violently. Television entertains them with real, violent police chases and shoot-outs, not to mention something that passes for professional wrestling but is nothing more than violence as entertainment. Lest we forget, the genre of point and shoot video games literally condition kids to kill. For further information on this, I highly recommend a book by Colonel David Grossman, Stop Teaching Our Kids To Kill. It is excellent.

You may say, "Well, Bill, you played cops and robbers, as well as war games when you were a kid," and yes, I did. But, my generation was not immersed in the graphic violence of today. Furthermore, our parents were "around" us to limit our exposure.

We were driving through South Georgia one day and the car in front of us hit a cow damaging the car and severely injuring the cow. Hit a cow? Yes, hit a cow! My Dad made me put my head down and close my eyes. He did not want me to see a cow suffering. Violence to him and his generation was not a spectator sport. They had seen enough blood in places like Normandy, Iwo Jima, and Okinawa. Death was not funny.

The truly terrifying aspect of the violence revolution is the fact that totally innocent and uninvolved people can become its victims by simply being in the right place at the wrong time. Think back to the school massacres covered by the media. The real victims were where they were supposed to be: in school classrooms.

Why Do Kids ...?

When we ask ourselves why kids become drawn to the Toxic Culture, our first thoughts usually run to peer pressure ... a desire to feel good ... a desire to escape ... a desire to rebel and similar sentiments. While these desires may be connected to their actions, I think the basic attractions of the Toxic Culture were described, in the 1940's, by a psychologist involved in research that had no direct connection with today's Toxic Culture. That psychologist was Dr. Abraham Maslow. His goal was to find out why people make the decisions they make and, in the process, reveal why people choose to buy any given product.

Maslow identified five basic needs that we all must meet. The critical distinction here is between wants and needs. While a want is something you would like to have, a need is something you must have. Let me make it clear that Dr. Maslow never intended for his research to be applied directly or indirectly to the drug culture; nonetheless, his findings apply. After we have identified the five needs all of us share, we can then explore the perverted ways in which the Toxic Culture meets these needs for children.

Maslow's Hierarchy Of Needs

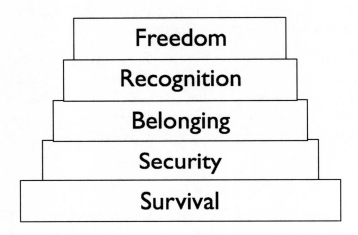

Survival — The first need Dr. Maslow identified as a reason to buy was survival. I have to live. There are certain things I must have in order to live. I have to have food; I must have clothing; I must have shelter. I need these things because all are essential to survival.

Safety — Dr. Maslow said, once my survival needs are met, my concerns shift and focus on safety. I need to feel secure in my environment; I need to know that someone is not going to break into my home; I need to feel that I am safe from attack. So, I am motivated to take whatever actions I believe will secure my safety.

Love — The third reason to buy, according to Dr. Maslow, is the need for Love - intimacy. Remember that the needs he is identifying are not my preferences or things I might possibly like to have; he is identifying critical needs.

"Intimacy" is not the exact word Dr. Maslow used to label our third need. To be precise, he used the phrase "love and belonging." He clarified the phrase by saying it encompasses a sense of belonging to a group, a sense of being a part of something. I chose to use the word, "intimacy" because, in our culture, the word "love" has been extremely overused and often abused. I love my wife. I love my dog. I love hamburgers. I love baseball. But, by no means am I saying that I feel the same way about baseball as I do about my wife or my dog or my hamburgers. What Maslow is really saying about this third need is we feel a necessity to be close to somebody. We each need to have a best buddy, someone to whom we can open up, someone with whom we can share more than thoughts and facts. We need someone with whom we can comfortably share feelings, opinions, fears, and dreams. All of us need a sense of intimacy, that sense of sharing heart-to-heart, instead of just head-to-head.

Recognition — Once I have my need for intimacy secured, Dr. Maslow said, I focus on gaining recognition. You might also label the need appreciation or respect. Each of us must have an area in our lives where we are recognized as valuable, as "accomplished." This is a need we exhibit in the crib and carry with us to the grave. I have watched three-month-old babies, who have just learned to turn over, exhibit their new accomplishment again and again. Each time they look to the big folks in their world for recognition and praise. That need for recognition never goes away.

Recognition is a need that can sometimes be met in the simplest of ways. For example, I have always held that the greatest recognition center in any young child's life is the refrigerator door. The drawing you display, the complimentary note from the teacher, the gold star for perfect attendance represent important recognition of your child's accomplishments and, above all your child's value to you, your family, and to your child's world.

As a youngster grows, he or she needs additional recognition, recognition from sources outside the home. The short list of time-honored organizations structured to give recognition is headed by the Boy Scouts and Girl Scouts of America. While I know that the Girl Scouts are as recognition-oriented as their counterpart, I can only speak from the personal perspective of a former Boy Scout. In the Scouts, if you burp, they put a merit badge on you. If you show up at the meeting, they hang a whistle on a rope around your neck. Kids thrive on recognition and proudly show up at meetings with their chests covered in badges, looking like General George Patton.

I will tell you how potent that recognition was to me; the Scouts are the only presence in the world that ever motivated me to clean a toilet. My mother never got me to do it. My wife never got me to do it. The Boy Scouts, however, had a merit badge called "Home Repairs," and part of the requirements for earning that badge included taking a toilet apart and cleaning it. The Scouts got me to do that because I wanted the associated merit badge; I needed that recognition. Indeed, if you have ever been around a military organization, you know people will literally risk their lives in battle for ribbons and metals. Recognition is that important to all of us in the human race.

Freedom — The fifth need identified by Dr. Maslow is self-actualization, Freedom, which might be translated as "Do your own thing." Self-actualization, as Maslow called it, is self-expression; it is becoming myself, in the fullest sense of the word; it is my attempt to fulfill my internal dream. For me to give up my dream would be to give up on myself. You are no different; neither is your child. A classic example of self-actualization is an experience I had in a clothing store. The best salesman I ever met showed me an outrageously expensive sports coat. It looked; it looked good on me. When I commented on how expensive it was, the salesman said, "Yes, but you deserve it."

I bought the coat. Not because he played on my needs for survival, safety, intimacy, or recognition, I bought it because he tapped my need for self-actualization. I needed that coat to fulfill my dream, to self-actualize. I simply owed it to myself.

Maslow Applied

Survival ... Safety ... Love ... Recognition ...Freedom. Those are the five needs that Dr. Abraham Maslow identified as being the reasons we make decisions, why we buy what we buy, why we use what we use, why we do what we do.

Let me again emphasize a critical point. These are needs... not wants. The child must meet these needs with something... with somebody... somehow.

Can you imagine a child using drugs for self-actualization purposes? Can you imagine children using drugs in order to feel they are doing their own thing? They do. That was the battle cry in the 1960's. If you can recall the introduction of marijuana and the coming out of the drug culture at Woodstock, the whole theme was break away, do your own thing, self-actualize, be free. So, self-actualization is a need that a kid can fill with ... among other things ... drugs. While some sought self-actualization turning on, tuning in, and dropping out, others took a 180 degree different path summed up in the U.S. Army slogan: be all that you can be.

Depending on from whom your child wants recognition, drugs and booze can assure he or she will be recognized. So can promiscuous sex. So can violence. "Look, there goes Billy Oliver. He's the Animal House of the high school. This guy can drink; you ought to see him put away the beer! Man, he was blitzed Saturday night." Maybe I'm not doing well in algebra. Maybe I'm not doing well in English. Maybe I'm not doing well at home. But, believe this: I am recognized by my teenage peers as somebody who at least does something well; I can party!

That same recognition through notoriety is applied to sexual promiscuity. "He's the stud of the campus." "She's ready to rock and roll." And, recognition also comes from staying in close proximity of violence. "He's cool, carries a knife" ... "keeps a 45 under the seat of his car" ... "nobody messes with him."

For some, violence also answers the need for distinction and recognition. According to Time Magazine, the boys who perpetrated the Columbine High School massacre in 1999 had as their goal to go down in history as the ultimate killers of all time. Yes, recognition comes from close association with drugs, sex, and violence.

And, what about intimacy? Does it link with the Toxic Culture? While promiscuous sex and intimacy seem at opposite ends of the pole, there is a link. It is the same as intimacy's connection with drugs and alcohol. Using drugs gains you acceptance with the group that is into drugs, into promiscuous sex, into even violence. However, the intimacy link does not necessarily involve all three.

I will never forget my daughter's words, when I asked her why she got involved with drugs. She said, "Dad, I would watch the drug users in the hall, and they just seemed to have more fun than the rest of the kids; so, I wanted to belong to that group."

A desire to belong, not peer pressure as conceived by adults, is the catalyst, the need. We adults tend to think of peer pressure as some third party going after our little darling. Kids literally laugh at that adult perception. In reality, it is our little darling wanting to be like the third party. True peer pressure is internal; it is the pressure we place on ourselves.

All of us place great importance on belonging. In fact, the adult alcohol use pattern at a cocktail party is a milder version of this need. We invite a group of people to our house. Most are strangers to one another. However, having something in their hands and being a part of an activity creates a common bond. At the same time, the alcohol in their glasses lowers anxiety levels to create a temporary feeling of comfort and belonging.

Can you imagine a child using alcohol or drugs for safety? After all, we know that abuse of drugs and alcohol can kill. So, why would a child use drugs or alcohol for safety? They do it to escape from the real world and feel safe for a little while. They do it to get away from the issues they do not wish to face. And, where do they learn that drugs can create a sense of safety? In many cases, they do not have to leave home to learn it. This Friday night, some young girl will be getting dressed to go to a party. She will be nervous. Her mom or dad will say, "No problem, take a couple of these to relax you. They're called Valium."

Yes, many times the child's first exposure to a mood altering drug is one that comes straight from the medicine cabinet in the child's own home. We think we are giving them relaxation, not drugs. But, the kids know as well as we do that a chemically induced state of relaxation creates a sense of safety. So, if two Valium are good, wonder what those little red pills those kids pop after school can do for me?

We have now worked our way back to the first need identified by Dr. Maslow: survival. Why would a child use alcohol or drugs for survival? Using drugs for survival is the very definition of an addict. At the addiction level, drugs and alcohol are no longer used for safety, for love and belonging, for recognition, for self-actualization, or even to party. In the addict's mind, the drug or alcohol is the very source of their survival. So, when you tell an addict, "Just say no," the picture in his mind is, "If I don't use this, I'm going to die." If you have ever gone through the experience of stopping smoking, you have had the thought: "I'll die without that cigarette." Take what you felt and multiple it by ten to approximate the desperation of a drug addict.

In a later chapter, we will examine the survival need and the virtually magnetic attraction between it and the Toxic Culture in much greater detail. For the moment, please just accept as fact that there is the thin line between social use and problematical use of drugs. Everything Dr. Maslow taught us about needs does apply to kids today.

Training Methodology

A key component is emersion in a culture is training. And, there is technology behind training. There is a distinct methodology, and when applied, it works. The airline pilot on the latest flight you took was trained in a video simulator. The soldiers who drive tanks and operate the other machinery and equipment of war are trained in simulators. So are our children. Go to any arcade in any shopping mall and you will see children in simulators, playing death games.

Arcade games and home computer games were originally very different from those out there today. Fifteen or twenty years ago, when the computerized arcade games were introduced, a friend of mine was baffled by the appeal cute little Pac Man and the antics of the Mario Brothers held for his twelve-year-old son. The boy explained it to him this way: "Dad, you like cartoons, don't you? So, here's your chance to be in one!"

Today's arcade games no longer concern themselves with ways of keeping the goofy little Mario Brothers from spilling a can of paint or getting a cute little cartoon monkey to the stalk of bananas he covets. Today's arcade games create amazingly realistic images that are often three dimensional. There is nothing inherently wrong with that. However, the games in the arcades and likely the video games in your home simulate death and destruction; they serve up violence and death as entertainment. Furthermore, they make the child playing the game into a simulated killer, all in the name of fun and entertainment.

Let me give you a personal and positive example of simulation. I recently abandoned the game of golf in respect for the sport. At approximately the same time, I happened to be flipping through the television channels and stopped at the one dedicated to fishing. That is when the idea of taking up fishing was planted in my head and somehow connected with thoughts I had never analyzed or verbalized. In other words, I bought into the idea that fishing might be FUN for me because I was open to a change.

I continued to watch, which farther stimulated my thinking. Next, I emulated a fisherman. In order to look like a fisherman, walk like a fisherman, talk and act like a fisherman, I bought all the hardware and software of the sport: the books, the rod, the reel, the clothing. After I acquired all the toys, I simulated being a fisherman. I assembled the equipment and practiced casting in the yard, practicing until I felt I understood what it would be like to catch a fish and stood a reasonable chance of doing just that. Next step: action. I went to a stream and gave it a try.

Stimulate, emulate, simulate, and act: those four steps are the same four taken in every adventure. The process is extremely predictable. A youngster watches a movie in which some kids go down a school hallway, wearing black trench coats and carrying shotguns, then proceed to blow away their classmates. Certainly every kid does not react in that way or find the idea appealing. However, for a certain percentage of the population (be it genetic, environmental, or whatever), they buy that idea. They buy it, just as a certain percentage of the population buys the idea of fishing, another percentage golf, and so on. After connecting with the idea that stimulates their thoughts, they emulate by acquiring the uniform and tools.

If all these steps feel good — and no one stops them — they move to the next level and simulate action. Kliebold and Harris, the Columbine Killers, practiced shooting in the nearby woods... and videoed the fun. You can count on what happened next because the process is perceived as fun. They Acted... they did the horrible thing... for FUN!

If you think I am over-reacting to the dangers of video game simulation, let me point out the observation of a military instructor who noted that the average person's firing pattern was to pull the trigger till the target falls. However, in massacres executed by kids, the firing pattern is very different. The firing pattern is the same taught for military combat and by video games: fire once and immediately move to the next target and the next and the next. That is the firing pattern used in every school massacre, shopping mall massacre, and street massacre I have been able to document.

The eight-year-old in his bedroom or the family den is learning those techniques right now with the aid of a video game, a television tube, and a joy stick. Furthermore, he is learning that violence and death are fun.

Socrates Sums It Up

Socrates said, if you wish to teach anything, create an environment in which the people you want to teach discover the truth for themselves. The same sort of self discovery Socrates advocated is what this book is about.

Consequently, it does not matter whether you agree with me or not. In fact, as you continue to read, there will likely be times you do not share my point of view. That is certainly acceptable to me because my purpose is to stimulate your thinking to the point that you realize (1) there is a Toxic Culture out there, (2) it holds powerful appeal, (3) it considers your child fair game, and most importantly, (4) you have the ability to rescue and/or protect your child from the fun and games of the Toxic Culture's drugs, promiscuous sex, and violence.

There is a well-known saying: "It takes a village to raise a child." I disagree and say that the village has proven itself incapable of the task. Today's village has an open sewer running through it... The Toxic Culture. Government, schools, civic and religious groups have a role and can help, but it is ultimately an obligation that parents must assume. Furthermore, the task cannot be left to the people most affected: the children. The inhabitants at Love Canal who took action were the parents. They did so because they were the ones with both the responsibility and the ability to protect their children.

Your situation is no different. Once again, it is parents who have the responsibility and the ability to protect today's children from the Toxic Culture. Now that we have defined the Toxic Culture, we will examine, in the chapters that follow, multiple ways in which you can take action to protect your child from this pervasive culture and see your child safely through adolescence into adulthood

CHAPTER THREE

PUT YOURSELF IN THE WAY

For the remainder of this book, we are going to use the acrostic P.A.R.E.N.T. as a memory tool, as a series of mental hooks on which we will hang important messages. Each letter will serve us as a guidepost, when steering your child clear of the Toxic Culture of drugs, sex, and violence. One chapter is dedicated to each letter. Let us begin by taking a brief look at what each of the letters represents.

Defining P.A.R.E.N.T.

The P in P.A.R.E.N.T. stands for Put Yourself in the Way. We are going to explore the importance of parents literally inserting themselves into the lives of their children.

The A stands for Awareness is Your Best Friend. Every parent has those little feelings that well up inside and signal something is not right here. In this chapter, you will acquire the skills needed to listen and respond affectively.

The R stands for Remember the Difference. There is a distinct difference between a child and an adult. Furthermore, an adolescent is neither one.

The E stands for Expect and Inspect. This chapter focuses on the importance of what your family believes and the importance of inspecting to see that you get what you expect.

The N stands for Never Give In.

The T, our final letter, stands for Traps to Avoid. The Toxic Culture sets traps for both you child and for you. Our final chapter helps you develop a route to follow, one that circumvents the traps and leads to the creation of family relationships you want and need.

A Teachable Moment For Me

The event that triggered the development of this chapter was a call I received from a long-time friend. When I answered the phone, this father got straight to the point: "Bill, we've got trouble with our son, Mark. He's run away from home."

I had worked in this field long enough to know, when a child runs away from home, you can suspect alcohol or drugs somewhere — not necessarily on the part of the child, but somewhere. Since I knew the parents were not involved with either, I said, "Well, you may have an alcohol or drug problem with Mark."

My friend could not accept the possibility that his seventeen-year-old son, who was a flanker on the football team, could be involved with either drugs or alcohol. So, I asked, "Then why did he run away from home?"

"Well," stammered the dad, " we wouldn't let him go to the rock concert."

Bingo! Alarms bells go off even louder.

Although Mark returned on his own, I took the parents out and talked with them. We talked, but not much penetrated their wall of denial. I will always regret that I did not push the issue hard enough, that I did not push it long enough. I did not because I hesitated to make them angry or hurt their feelings.

Three or four months later, I got another phone call from Mark's dad. "Bill, we've got terrible problems with Mark now." My immediate thoughts ran to breaking and entering, fake drivers license, automobile wreck; but it was much worse. "He's down at the county jail, and they're holding him for Murder One."

I had known this boy most of his life. I had known Mark as a toddler, played with him, held him in my arms. "My God, Fred, tell me what happened!"

There had been a party Saturday afternoon. The parents who lived at the party site were out of town. Mark and some of his friends started drinking about two o'clock in the afternoon. In addition to a well-stocked liquor cabinet, there were other drugs there: marijuana, maybe more. About five that afternoon, the neighbors complained to the police about the noise. When the police arrived, they told the boys to turn down the stereo and left. That the boys did, and the slightly less noisy party kept rolling.

About eight that night, at another house a couple of miles away, some parents were having a Sweet Sixteen Party for their daughter who attended a rival high school. Refreshments provided included kegs of beer. (Those parents later explained that they would rather their sixteen-year-old drink at home than drink somewhere else.) About half past nine, there was a phone call from the Sweet Sixteen Party to the boys' drinking bout. The call was from one of the boy's sister, saying, "I've been disrespected." Will you come over here and take care of it?"

Well, you know what "take care of it" means at ten at night to a group of kids who have been drinking. The guys loaded into their cars and headed for the Sweet Sixteen Party. As soon as they arrived, fights broke out. No one is certain how many were involved; estimates ranged from 150 to 200 kids. The girls were screaming, the guys were rolling around in the dirt, and all of a sudden a young man stood up. He has been stabbed, stabbed thirteen times around his front, around his side, and up his back.

An ambulance came, but it was too late; the boy died on the way to the hospital. When the police arrived at the party site, interviewed the kids, and asked if anyone saw somebody with a knife? "Yes," said some, "we saw Mark with a knife."

By the time the police interviewed Mark, he was in an alcoholic blackout. This is a state you may never have witnessed. While most of us have seen someone who has passed out, a blackout is quite different. A blackout is when a person has consumed an enormous amount of alcohol; however, the body does not shut down and go into sleep mode… it is more like sleepwalking.

The person experiencing blackout can still walk and talk, even perform some fairly complex skills. Nonetheless, a person in this state is later unable to remember anything done or said. Pilots have successfully flown airplanes in an alcoholic blackout, not remembering the takeoff or the landing. That was Mark's condition. He could not defend himself and admitted to having a knife. Because of the witnesses who said they saw him with a knife and his admission of ownership, Mark was arrested, jailed, and charged with Murder One.

His parents hired an attorney and, after spending thousands of dollars — not to mention experiencing profound misery — the lawyer's negotiations resulted in getting the plea reduced from Murder One to Voluntary Manslaughter. Seventeen year-old Mark was sentenced to twenty years in a state prison.

This is what happened to a good kid. If you had met Mark a year or so before the incident, you would have said, "I'd like to have a son like him."

But, that is not the end of the story. The story's real tragedy was revealed when the press came and interviewed the parents of the sixteen-year-old who was celebrating her birthday. The press asked: "Where were you when all of this was happening in your front yard?"

The parents replied, "We were upstairs, trying to stay out of the way."

My Parents Are Wacko

But, our job as parents is to stay in the way, firmly entrenched between the Toxic Culture and our children. Later, when you are old, when you are in the retirement home, they will love you for it. But, during this adolescent passage, when the allure of the Toxic Culture is so strong, you should be in their environment and literally be in the way, whether your intervention is welcomed or not.

Here is an example of that. Have you ever had your child receive a phone call and heard: "Oh, sure, I'd love to spend the night at your house." Then you child asked: "Mom, may I go over to Kelly's house and spend the night?" All the time that she was asking permission, the child was shaking her head, "NO!"

Think about what was said and what was asked. What was your child doing? She was using you as an excuse to say "No."

We say to our kids, "Just say no," without giving them a reason. So, our children fill in a reason that makes sense to them and sense to their peers. They deduce: "I have a wacko mother or father. I would love to party with you guys but my dad's a nut. My mom is a kook."

Kids feel a deep need to give their peers a valid reason, one that also lets them off the hook. They need a reason because we have taught them from birth not to just say "no." We have taught them it is impolite; you always give a reason. To save face with one's peers, it has to be a reason that is beyond the giver's control. "I can't come because I'm sick" ... "because my parents are nuts" ... "because the house is on fire."

It can not be an excuse that involves any fault or shortcoming in either the person giving the excuse or the one receiving it. No self-respecting kid is going to say: "I suspect there will be drugs at the party" ... "I think you'll pressure me to have sex" ... "You drive like a maniac." Therefore, our job as moms and dads, in many instances, is to be our children's reason to say "no." Every kid deserves a "Wacko" parent.

The "A" List

When the Toxic Culture reaches out to your child, there are numerous actions you can take that will put you in the way and create a protective barrier. The following is a list of steps you can take that will go a long way toward helping your child get safely through the adolescent passage. The steps will be easy to recall because the key word in each begins with the letter A.

The first is Be **Aware** of Your Child's Attitudes. Watch your children. Ask yourself: what is this child buying into and communicating? Go sit in your child's room. You are not there to check for dust and dirty socks. Also, you are not there to search the room ... although I do not think that is necessarily a bad idea.

But, do go sit in your child's room. Take a pad and a pen with you. Pretend you never met this child and, based upon what you see on the walls, write down the attitude of the person who lives in that room. Do not do this just once; I suggest you go through the exercise about every sixty days. If you notice a change in the

---

42

attitude the room reveals, a red flag should go up in your mind, and you should take action.

Second, Be **Around** Your Child's Activities. Show up. Start doing it at a very young age. Set the precedent in your family that when your children are ten, eleven, and twelve years of age, you show up at the parties they attend. When they are fourteen and fifteen, continue showing up. If you do, when they are fifty, they will still be looking over their shoulder for you to come up that driveway.

What does this do for them? At times, it may irritate them. At times, they may be less than thrilled to see you pop in. But, the fact that you frequently do and just might any second gives them an excuse to say no. "I'd love to party, but my dad may show up. And, let me tell you, if my dad shows up, I'll be in Big-time trouble!"

Third, Be **Aware** of Your Child's Environments. Your child's environments are radically different from those you grew up in. For example, I grew up in the days when the most scandalous movie on the silver screen was The Outlaw, a cowboy movie about Billy the Kid and Doc Holliday. My mama would not let me go see it for the same reason none of my friends' parents would not let them see it.

The ruckus was over a single scene that, by today's standards, is pretty tame. In that infamous scene, Jane Russell reclines seductively in a haystack. As she does, the camera moves in to show about an inch of….. cleavage. The music goes dum de dum dum dum, and they cut to the corral. That was the scene, and America was up in arms about that. The movie was even banned in Boston.

I wanted to see The Outlaw, but Mamma absolutely would not let me. Furthermore, I did not see it until a few years ago. I was walking through K-Mart, spotted a copy of the film on video tape, bought it, and took it home. There is nothing in it. There is more sex and violence on Saturday morning cartoons than there was in that movie. Nonetheless, I was shocked. I was astounded at how entertainment for kids has changed.

I teach a senior high Sunday school class. At a point when attendance started to lag, I told the kids, "Next Sunday, I'm going to show you what was considered an X-rated movie when I was your age. But you have to promise not to tell anybody."

Attendance tripled. The next Sunday, I closed the door, closed the blinds, and said, "Okay, we're going to see a movie that was literally considered pornography when I was a kid." I added, "If this will embarrass anybody, if you feel like you're going to be hurt by this, just raise your hands and we'll let you leave. We won't hold it against you."

One little girl, sitting in the back raised her hand. I asked, "Honey, would you like to leave?"

She said, "I can't see the screen. May I come up front?"

So, I showed The Outlaw. At the end of the infamous scene, I stopped the video tape and said, "That's it."

They said, "That's what?"

"That's the scene our parents wouldn't let us see."

They said, "You've got to be kidding. Can we see that again?"

I showed those teenagers that scene about four times. They were shocked to learn that was ever a bad movie.

I learned something about kids that day. Kids think today has always been. They draw a trend line through one data point, and they say today has always been.

I then asked them what movies they had seen recently? Their honest answers included a string of R-rated films. "Okay," I said, "if my mamma wouldn't let me see The Outlaw and you're going to see movies that are filled with sex, violence, and drugs, what do you think the movies will be like when your kids grow up?"

Their reply was, "Oh, they're really going to be bad." You know, kids are pretty smart.

Then I said, "Let me ask you a question. Which movie do you want your children to see?" Their answer was The Outlaw. They did not want their children seeing the movies they were seeing.

Let us continue our list of A's. Fourth is Be **Assertive** in Your Parenting. I am absolutely convinced that we have become a nation of parental wimps, that we are literally nerds when it comes down to being a mom and being a dad. We are so afraid that we are not going to be liked by our children. At the same time, we tell them, "Just say no," we are afraid to say "no" ourselves.

Your child is not going to break. Your child is not going to shatter. I think I raised my older daughter as though she was so fragile. She is not. She is a very, very resilient person. She can come back from some tremendous ordeals. Your child is not fragile, either. Be assertive in your parenting.

I want parents to do the same thing that non-smokers did. When the Surgeon General first came out with his report that said cigarettes cause cancer, we did absolutely nothing. We took the position that as long as it does not affect me, whatever you do is your decision.

A number of years later, the Surgeon General came out with a second report that said the breathing of second-hand smoke by non-users causes cancer. That is when we began passing laws and enforcing them. It happened when the non-users realized they were the victims.

So, who are the victims of drugs? The victims are kids who do not use drugs and the families of drug users. In my opinion, drug users — particularly the adult drug users — are not victims. They are part of the conspiracy because they finance the drug cartel. To rid ourselves of the danger drug users pose to all of us, we must look upon the fall-out from their activities as being a hazard to our well-being.

Be assertive in your parenting. I assure you the drug culture is assertive in its recruiting process.

Finally, Be **Awake** When Your Child Comes Home. One of the greatest drug prevention tools in the world is moms and dads, standing at the door when children come in from a date or a party. Open that door. Hug them. Be there to look them in the eye. Tell them you love them and are glad they are back.. When you do these things, you are also there to smell their breath and check their pupils. That sort of parenting gives a kid a solid excuse to say "No!" The parents of my generation certainly did.

When my wife of 54 years... (That right... 54... I have earned the right to call this book LESSONS LEARNED)... and I were dating, the driveway of her family's house lead around back to a garage. At night, that end of the driveway was wrapped in shadows. One evening, as I arrived to take Vicky to a movie, I discovered her dad on a stepladder, mounting a spotlight on the garage. "Hey, Mr. M," I said, "what are you doing?"

He replied, "You'll find out later."

When we returned and brought the car to a stop in the shadows, after about five minutes, the new spotlight went blink, blink, and blink. Not sure exactly what that meant, we continued our stay in the car. In another couple of minute, the spotlight blinked twice and stayed on. In short order, Vicky's dad came out of the house, walked down the driveway, opened the car door, and escorted his daughter inside. That, my friends, is first-rate parenting.

You may not share my comfort level with such a degree of involvement and wonder: "How will my child feel about having a super protective wacko for a parent?"

That same question came to my mind and caused me great concern over how our younger daughter, Julie, would react. She never became involved with drugs. But, because I was so wrapped up in drug prevention, I wondered if my attitudes and actions might warp her? Would the kids give her a hard time? I really worried about that.

The day before Julie left for college, she called me at the office and asked if we could have lunch together. Well, I thought, here it comes. She wants a car. She's gotten everything else.

At lunch, she surprised me. "Dad," she said, "I want to say two things. First, I want to thank you, and second, I want to apologize to you."

"Well, I can understand why you want to thank me, but why would you want to apologize to me?"

This was her answer: "Dad, during my high school career, I've said some things about you that really aren't true. I said them because I needed a reason to say 'No.' I've told people I'd love to party, but you know my daddy; he's a real wacko on the subject." I smiled, and she continued: "I realize now that I'm going off to college, I no longer have you as an excuse."

The Image

Let me give you the image that I would like to plant in your mind; it happened at Tiananmen Square in China. Although the event took place several years back, I am sure you remember seeing it on television.

The tanks were coming down the street, and the students who were protesting for their freedom filled the Square. The camera zoomed in on a Chinese student with an umbrella. He walked out in front of a tank and planted himself squarely in its path. The tank rolled right up to the young man and stopped. After a few moments, the tank moved to the right. The student moved to the right. The tank stopped. The tank moved to the left; so, the student moved to the left, and there was a standoff. Suddenly, the student crawled up on the tank, rapped on the hatch, and had a conversation with the driver.

That is putting yourself in the way. And, doing that takes courage. It is not easy, but you can and will have to do it. You will have the courage to put yourself between your child and the Toxic Culture because you are a parent, and putting yourself in the way is in your job description. It is part of The Deal

CHAPTER FOUR

AWARENESS IS YOUR BEST FRIEND

In the previous chapter, we introduced the acrostic, P.A.R.E.N.T. The P, as you recall, stands for Put Yourself in the Way. We now move to the A, which stands for Awareness Is Your Best Friend. In this chapter, you are shown how a child becomes a product of the Toxic Culture and how to determine if your child is involved in that culture.

How to Make a Pickle

We know that drugs, alcohol, sex, and violence are not new. So, how have they become an integral part of our children's lives? Perhaps I can answer that by posing what may seem a frivolous question: How do you make a pickle? To make one, you start with a cucumber. Then you place the cucumber into a mixture of vinegar, salt, and spices.

In other words, you immerse the cucumber into a culture. If you quickly take the cucumber out of the culture, you still have a slightly wet but still fresh cucumber. However, if you let it sit there, if you leave it in the culture long enough, you will end up with a pickle.

You might ask how long does it take to make a pickle? The answer is: it varies. Some cucumbers become pickles early, some become pickles late. But, left in the culture long enough, eventually all cucumbers will become pickles.

Extend that idea and ask yourself: how do you make a doctor? You take a young person of talent and ability and send her to school. You send her to college, then medical school… a culture of "medical". Next follows an internship at a hospital, then a formal residency… more intense medical cultures. After a number of years, you have yourself a physician.

You make a lawyer in a similar way; you send him to law school… a legal culture.

You make a policeman by sending him to the police academy… a police culture.

To make a plumber, you apprentice a young person in a plumbing culture.

So, how do you make a drug user? How do you make a sexually promiscuous kid? How do you make a kid who walks into a school, puts fellow schoolmates behind the site of a gun, and pulls the trigger when one answers in the affirmatively to the question: "Do you believe in God?"

It is so very easy.

You allow that youngster to become immersed in America's Toxic Culture. When you do, it transforms children's minds because we have defined, for our them, promiscuous sex, drugs, violence, and death as entertainment… as pleasant… as FUN!

I want to walk you through the steps a child takes in order to grow a full-blown state of addiction, which left untreated, Kills. To do that, I employ the time-honored analogy of a ladder.

You see only the top of the ground. But, the real action is taking place on the lower rungs. The first Step is a Thought. Imagine a cutaway view of the soil of that young mind. It is rich. It is fertile. New thoughts can easily sprout there.

The process starts with the planting of a single thought in the fertile mind of your child. Where do thoughts come from? For example, where would your child get the thought that it might be okay to use alcohol and drugs or take part in after-school orgies? Or to carry a gun to school.

Thoughts do not materialize out of thin air. They are stimulated by something. That's what the Advertising Industry does for a living... plant thoughts.

In my seminars, I asked the parents " Where do thoughts come from?"

The first answer I invariably hear is "television." Sure. One of the biggest teachers in America today is television. The movies are usually the second source of thoughts mentioned. But, let's not beat TV and the movies to death. There are other sources. If we are being honest with ourselves, we have to include their friends' behavior and their parents' behavior. We also have to list our schools and neighbors.

If I made the list, I would place Hollywood near the top, with its "party till you puke" philosophy. Youngsters at any point in time seem to believe that the music of their day is more relevant, more worthy than all the melodies and lyrics that came before their time. The problem is today's music is not about puppy love, holding hands, and stealing a kiss. If you really do not know what today's music is saying, you need to listen. While you are at it, pay close attention to the songs that are not aired on the radio.

Developing A Belief System

Take a hard look at some of these influences that are seeding our children's value systems. On television, premarital sex is honored as the norm. Remember FRIENDS? It is what regular folks are supposed to do. Unwed mothers are virtually deified. They are usually shown as brave, self-sufficient towers of strength and respectability. Programs, such as Entertainment Tonight glory in serving up titillating stories of who is sleeping with whom and who just had another illegitimate child by whom. To hear such reports equates Fathers Day in Hollywood and the sports world with mass confusion.

Also, there are the stories the magazine format shows love to report about how this celebrity or that has shaken drugs or alcohol, coming out of the situation with absolutely no negative effects. A child watching unsupervised television can see at least five simulated murders a night, not counting the real ones the news media salivates over.

The movies are as bad or worse when it comes to glorifying the toxins in our culture. If you wonder why teens today have such foul mouths, check out a few cool flicks that the critics raved about and count the four-letter words. I counted the cutely-dubbed "F Bomb" 73 times in one movie that was a big favorite of teens. The film's running time is less than two hours; so, that works out to over one Bomb" every two minutes. I did not realize that the F Word could be used as a noun, a verb, and an adjective in the same sentence. While I will concede that an occasional bit of profanity is a part of realism, we just do not need that much of it to make a point in films aimed at any audience.

One of these days, I am going to order refreshments with the same words used in the films. "I'd like a F...ing bag of F...ing popcorn and a F...ing small F...ing drink." Maybe that's why my beautiful wife goes shopping instead seeing the movie.

Don't get me wrong. I like going to the movies, at least going to some of them. One of my favorite films is E.T. I do not think there has been a cuter, cuddlier character created by the entertainment industry.

As appealing as that movie is, there is a scene in E.T. that deeply disturbs me: the one that sells the benefits of getting drunk. Let me re-create the scene for you. The little alien E.T. is at the home of his eight-year-old earth buddy Elliot, while Elliot is at school.

Remember that the two have touched fingers, enabling them to share thoughts and feelings.

At home, with nothing to do, E.T. becomes bored and heads for the kitchen. He opens the big white box his earth hosts call "the refrigerator," reaches in, pulls out a can of beer, and drinks it. It's pretty good stuff. So, he drinks another, proceeds to get cute, giggly drunk, and trashes the house. E.T.'s and Elliot's ability to share feelings then comes into play; at school, Elliot also becomes cute, giggly drunk.

It was a very funny scene; we all laughed. But, it should be very sobering to any parent to realize that this cute experience carried with it absolutely no negative consequences. I wish they had shown E.T. throwing up. I wish they had shown him O.D. I wish they had shown him having to have his stomach pumped. But, they did not.

The experience was packaged as great fun. Consequently, every eight-year-old in America learned from that movie that he or she can get drunk without paying any penalty whatsoever. Furthermore, getting drunk is kind of cute; after all, E.T. did it.

That is not an isolated example. You remember how the Disney character Dumbo learned to fly?

The roustabouts at the circus, where the little elephant lived, got him drunk. And while Dumbo was drunk, he learned to fly. Courage from a bottle proved to be the catalyst for Dumbo's accomplishments and success. My point is this: G-Rated does not necessarily mean Non-Toxic.

You and I cannot insulate our children from thoughts. We could lock them in the attic, but that is not our goal — much less a workable solution. Nor can we pre-screen every movie and TV show they see or shield them from the behavior of neighbors, family, and friends. To better understand our realistic options, consider what takes place in the mind of a child. A thought being planted in the child's mind is the starting point. The next thing that happens in the child's head is that thought spouts. It gets considered. The child plays that thought on the screen of the mind.

"What would it be like if I did what E.T. did?" And he or she visualizes being E.T. If the result of that consideration is pleasure, your child will probably do what E.T. did. If, on the other hand, the result of playing that thought on the screen of the mind is pain or fear of getting caught, your child probably would not do it.

While that is what is taking place, you simply will not know how the thought is being processed. Not, at least, during the sprouting process. As time progresses, the sprouted thought develops roots, and those roots produce an attitude. Once that attitude germinates and breaks the surface of the mind's soil, you can then see it.

Attitudes that sprout can range from "being an archeologist is cool" to "drugs are cool" to "group sex is cool." No matter what the decision, an alert parent who knows what to look for can see greater and greater evidence of a whole new attitude. If you are trying to comfort yourself with the notion that negative attitude and negative action are two separate things, I am about to ruin your day. They are inseparably linked. The simple truth is an attitude is nothing more than pre-packaged decision ready to happen. After anyone adopts an attitude about something, if he or she ever gets the chance, that person is going to do it, whatever "it" might be.

I tell you this as a business man: if I can get you, your child, anyone to wear my tee-shirt, you will buy my product when you get the money. If I can get you to put my name on your chest, whenever you can afford it, you are going to own my product. So, what does your child's favorite tee-shirt depict? What does it say? Does it say your child is gravitating toward an attitude that is pro-alcohol, pro-party, pro-drugs, pro-violence? He is wearing a billboard that spells out a new attitude for all to see. She is telling the world that what she used to think of as bad and horrible is now, in her mind, acceptable. Even desirable.

There are other pronouncements of a new attitude in the rest of your children's wardrobes. Take notice of whom they emulate in their choice of clothes. Is it a gangster look that some fringe rock group sports? Is it the look favored by the older kids who gravitate towards trouble? Is it gang colors? Is it Goth? What exactly is the "uniform" your children are attempting to emulate?

Your child's wardrobe is not the only billboard on which he or she spells out new attitudes. They are also plastered on the walls of your child's room. Exactly how is that room decorated? What is on those walls? If you walked into my house, I guarantee you could take a hard look at the walls of my family room and tell what the attitudes are in our house. Furthermore, I am convinced I could walk into your house and tell you a lot about yourself and your attitudes, based on the articles you incorporate into your home's decor. Just as we spell out our attitudes, so do our children. Someone wise once said, "Looking is not seeing." That is correct. You have to pay attention to what you are looking at in order to see it for what it is.

Another pronouncement of changing attitudes is choice of friends. With whom are they choosing to run? What does that crowd believe? There is an old saying: if it looks like a duck, and walks like a duck, and quacks like a duck, it's probably a duck. Are your children's friends ducks? If so, you probably have one living under your roof, as well.

Body language also speaks volumes. How do they react to authority figures? Whose mannerisms do they ape? Do their eyes glaze over when you are trying to talk to them? The point is, through body language, dress, the world they create within their living space, and their choice of friends, they are shouting their attitudes at you. Literally shouting.

If, as I stated earlier, attitude is a pre-packaged decision waiting for the opportunity to be put it into action, the next step is, of course, the action. After the attitude sprouts, as soon as conditions are favorable, action follows. We all operate in that way. I may well develop an attitude two years before I take the action. I have attitudes about many things that I just cannot afford to act on. But, when I get the chance to act on my attitudes, I take the action. We all do.

After we live with an action long enough, it becomes a habit. A habit is nothing more than an automatic action. After you or I have done something many times, we no longer have to think about it; the action becomes automatic. For instance, when we first started learning to tie our shoes, we had to think about it. We had to think long and hard about every loop, twist, and turn. But, I doubt you have not given the process of tying your shoes real thought in twenty years. You no longer think about it because it is habit; it is routine; it is now a part of you. While tying your shoes is a good habit, the process for developing a bad one is no different. Consequences, however, are where the difference comes into play.

When you live with any habit that involves a toxic substance or toxic life style long enough, you develop an addiction. That is a law of nature. So, the question becomes: how do we prevent the planting of undesirable thoughts that can grow into attitudes ... attitudes that, in turn, mutate into actions ... then into habits ... then into addictions?

Playing in the Sewer

We are allowing our children to play in the Toxic Culture's Sewer. If you are going to intervene in your child's life, first you need to minimize his or her exposure to the messages of the Toxic Culture. Kids do not need to see everything. Kids do not need to hear everything. Kids do not need to be exposed to every thought and lifestyle in the world. But, the fact is you are not going to be fully aware of everything they are exposed to until you spot evidence that some thought has sprouted, taken root, and is growing an attitude.

Nonetheless, the logical first step is to prevent as many negative ideas as possible from sprouting by putting distance between them and your child. That takes intervening in your child's life. That takes keeping children, whenever possible, from playing in the sewer. As best you can, control their world. Control what they watch on TV, control what movies they see. Control what they are allowed to wear. Control with whom they are allowed to spend time.

Your attempts at controlling will not complete the job. Despite your best efforts, toxic ideas will find their way into your child's mind. Be on the look-out for the slightest manifestation of a new attitude that you cannot condone. The minute you see your child buying into something that is new, strange and negative, address it. Address it by saying something similar to this: "Kevin, that attitude is unacceptable in this family, and we're not going to have it. It really hurts me to see that."

It is that simple. Speak up. Speak loud. Speak often. Let them know you stoutly stand by your belief system, are not shy about expressing it, and take pride in your beliefs and standards. If you do not have what it takes to stand up for your beliefs, how can you expect a kid to stay on track?

Remember, to tolerate an idea or a behavior is to teach it.

Now or Later

At some point in time, you are going to "intervene"; you are going to get between your child and the Toxic Culture. It may be at the attitude stage, or it may be as late at the addiction stage. But, at some point, you will place yourself squarely between your child and the Toxic Culture. Let us say the issue is drugs. The easiest time to intervene is the moment your child becomes aware that there are such things as drugs. It is easier to have ten minutes of hassle now than wait five years and then face a lifetime of hassle. When that toxic thought in your child's mind is young, when its roots are not mature, when they have not gone down deep into the soil of your child's mind to thrive on your child's intellect, will, and emotions, that is the time to do it.

The Toxic Culture impact starts with the planting of a single thought. And what do you think that thought is? "I can handle it. It won't happen to me."

Every child I have ever talked to in treatment never thought it would happen to them. Nor did the parents. In his or her head, the child thinks: "Oh, I'll drink this, but I'll never use that. I'll snort this, but I'll never inject that. I'll do this, but I'll never end up in treatment... or jail... or dead." Unfortunately, that is not how it works. Once a child reaches the addiction stage, there must be three to six months of hard work just to attack that root thought: I can handle it. It won't happen to me. Until that thought changes, there is no recovery. That is the very reason that Alcoholics Anonymous has as its first step, "I admit that I am powerless over drugs and alcohol. I cannot handle them."

Intervention Versus Prevention

Frankly, I'm not sure we can prevent drug use. The word prevention carries with it the concept of holding someone back. The image I would rather have you adopt is I am coming between the drugs and my child just as I would come between them and a rattlesnake encountered in the woods. If you saw that your child's path was about to intersect with that of a rattler, you would not run out of the way. You would literally put your body between the two. You would intervene. That is the image that we want. If you are going to prevent Toxic Behaviors, it starts with minimizing thoughts and addressing each negative attitude the instant you sense its presence.

The Alarm Bell Is Ringing

Every parent has a God-given, built-in alarm bell. Sometimes it seems that bell goes off with no provocation. Try as we may, we cannot put our finger on what is wrong. Nonetheless, down deep we know something is not the way it should be or used to be. Some people call it intuition. Some people call it instinct. Some call it inspiration. I think what is really happening is not quite that mysterious or exotic. For example, you probably know your child as well or better than anyone on the face of the earth. The alarm bell sounds when you are receiving facts and information you do not know how to translate or interpret. Still, the information is reaching your subconscious mind, causing the alarm bell to sound. You know how your child looks and acts when she is well. Therefore, when she is not well, you spot a difference. You may not know if the problem is a cold, measles, influenza, or a host of other ailments; however, you spot symptoms.

Spotting symptoms of illness in your child is demanded of you by law. In a Supreme Court decision, it was established that there are only three compelling situations in which the State can come between you and your family: when you (1) abuse your child; (2) neglect your child; or (3) abandon your child. In a subsequent case, in which the parents were forcing their child to attend church, the Court ruled that the parents had that right because neither abuse, neglect, or abandonment were involved; therefore, the Court could not interfere.

The law's definition of neglect includes medical neglect. The law demands that you, as a parent, be responsible for spotting symptoms of disease and obtaining medical attention for your child. But, when the symptoms of our child's involvement in the Toxic Culture surface, we rationalize that alarm bell. We comfort urselves by mouthing one or more of the following fatal paradigms. I ask you to study the following list of Fatal Paradigms.

It's just a phase and will pass.

Alcohol, pot and etc. are no big deal.

There is nothing I can do about it.

It's a right of passage.

Let them decide for themselves.

It won't happen to me.

All the kids are doing it.

I did it when I was growing up.

My kids won't listen to me.

I don't have time.

The School will handle that.

Any one of the above reactions constitutes denial. It is turning a deaf ear to your alarm bell, which is your great ally in the struggle to get your child safely through the adolescent passage. Do not muffle that bell, do not ignore it. When it rings, it is ringing for a reason.

Spotting the Real Thing

How would you know if your child is becoming toxic? Perhaps an analogy can help us find the answer. Let us say you go to work for a bank. One of the first things you would learn is how to distinguish real money from counterfeit money. As a teller, you would be taught the difference. You would be taught to know the real thing very intimately, very closely. You would learn what the real thing feels like. What it looks like. The characteristics of the paper. The true colors of the inks. The smallest details in the printing. As a teller, you would be around real money all day long and develop an instinctive knowledge about what is real and what is counterfeit.

Like the people in the banking business, my approach is to start by teaching you how to tell the real child from the toxic counterfeit through comparison. The counterfeit may, at first glance, look real, but comparison reveals there is something wrong, something not quite right, something you can learn to identify. Let's begin by recalling how a child develops.

When a child is only days old, she begins developing a concept of self. Babies in their cribs, examining their fingers and toes, know when they are hungry, when they are uncomfortable, when they are wet. In its tiny crib world, each child begins developing a sense of self. I am somebody. Within the first few weeks, babies learn to use their eyes well enough to look beyond their cribs. At that point, they begin to recognize family. Although tiny, the babies understand they have a different relationship with each of the big folks who come around. Infants might not know names, such as Mom or Dad or Sis, but they quickly learn who shows them love and in what ways they show it.

The development continues. At about age four or five, we introduce children to a concept called "school." That is when they learn there is more to life than Teletubbies, Barney, Big Bird, and playing with blocks on the family room floor. There are other kids out there. Bunches of them. A child absolutely thrives in that nursery school and kindergarten environment. In what seems like minutes to us adults, instead of years, they are ten, eleven, twelve, thirteen, and they seem to go crazy. At some point, friends become overwhelmingly important to the child. All of a sudden it is no longer so much self, family and school, life now revolves around their BFF's. Even though they see that best friends for six or seven hours at school, what is the first thing they do when then come home? Your daughter or son heads for the phone and calls that best friend. When you say get off the phone, the best friend calls back. The two of them would talk all night, if you would let them. Friends become overwhelmingly powerful once the child begins developing a sense of activities. As the television series The Wonder Years summed up this chapter in life, "After all, in middle school, you are who you eat lunch with." Developing a sense of Personal Interests does not necessarily link with choice of best friend. They are two separate things that occur at about the same time in life. While one can influence the other, there is not an inseparable link. This business of developing Personal Interests has to do with preparing themselves for life. Hobbies, sports, Boy Scouts, Girl Scouts, choir, activities all have a sense of the future. The child is testing options and planning. "What am I going to be when I grow up?" And they start to talk about, "Well, I want to be a football player," or "I want to be a doctor," or "I want to be a lawyer," or "I want to be a teacher." A sense of future begins, and that is normal development you can expect to see in the emotionally healthy child. That is the real child, and understanding first what is real helps us spot the counterfeit.

As the child becomes more and more toxic, the Child begins to shrink from the outside in:

Activities/Interests Change.

Friends Change.

School Performance Drops.

Family Relationships Begin To Fall Apart.

The Child Develops A Bad Self Image.

The child has to rearrange his or her life in order to accommodate the Toxic Culture, which eventually demands more and more of two things: time and money. So, as the rearrangements progress, the aware parent notices changes in patterns and activities. Billy is no longer going to choir practice. The parent asks: "Billy, are you going to choir practice?" "No." "Why not?" "Well, it's boring."

It's Boring

When you hear the word "boring", stop dead in your tracks. When you hear "School is boring, the teacher is boring, you are boring, this family is boring, this house is boring, this town is boring," remember: "boring" is a comparative term. When your child says "boring", he is comparing what he has in front of him to something else he would rather have or do. She is making a judgement call. So, whenever you hear the word, "boring," I want you to say this: "Compared to what?"

Ask and keep asking until you have the truth. The truth may not be an answer you want to hear, but you need to keep pushing until you know the question has been truthfully answered. What you may learn is that your child is shifting activities to those areas where he or she can "party" and be around people who "party."

Let's define that word. In the Toxic Culture, "party" does not equal playing pin the tail on the donkey or dancing; it is getting high and/or having sex. Such a party can involve as few as two people or as many as you can count. "Party" is a verb, not a noun in the Toxic Culture. We used to have a party. Kids today "party", with sex, drugs, and a potential for violence.

Still, it may not yet be time to panic. Remember I said earlier that kids first buy into the Toxic Culture, then, after a certain time, they get into the activities of that culture. They first buy into a lifestyle, but participation comes later. How much later is hard to say. It can be days, weeks, months, even years. But, when they start rearranging and eliminating activities to keep company with the Toxic Culture, you need to start being concerned about that. Listen when the alarm bell sounds, be concerned and investigate — but do not panic.

If you let the matter slide and your child starts rearranging friendships so that he or she can run with those kids who make up the toxic crowd, you will soon have a conversation that sounds like this: "Are you going out with John tonight?" "No." "Well, you haven't seen John in a long time; don't you like John anymore?" "No, he's boring."

Compared to what? Compared to what!? If you child is unwilling to give you a truthful and complete answer, you must keep persisting until you realize what the answer truly is.

One phenomenon you can look to as a clear sign is toxic kids generally do not like to run with straight kids. And, kids who are straight generally do not like to run with the toxic kids.

So, be on guard when you will find your child gravitating towards a group of friends you do not know. "Whom are you going out with tonight?" "Well, I'm going out with Bubba." "Who's Bubba?" "Well, you don't know him." "What's Bubba like?" "You wouldn't be interested, Mom. He's a nice guy, very nice guy, really a nice guy." "Then invite him over." "No, that's not a good idea; he's not comfortable around adults."

When children run around with people you do not know or they run around with kids who you do not like, you have a legitimate reason not to like them. The reason is, in those other children, you see what may well be developing in your child.

One of the mistakes that you can make and one of the mistakes that I made was saying to myself, "Well, my child is going to change those other kids for the good. My child is going to be a positive influence on them. She is going to lead them back out of the wilderness."

It seldom works that way. Author and lecturer Chuck Swindal hit the nail on the head with his explanation of the interaction between bad company and good morals. Swindal said, "If you take a white glove and you put it into a bucket of mud, the mud does not get glovey."

Bad joke, but it makes the point; if you allow your healthy child to enter the Toxic Culture, that culture will not become purified by your child's presence.

As you start to react to your child's friends, what you are really seeing — if you have the courage, wisdom, and love it takes to really look — is your child is becoming like them. You need to start being more concerned because big trouble is just around the corner.

The child develops difficulties at school. He becomes a discipline problem. She becomes a truant. He skips class or cut schools. Her grades drop. If your child is an A student his grades do not drop to Fs; they drop to Bs. If your child is a B student, grades drop to Cs. Cs drop to Ds. If your child has been struggling all along, he or she may start talking about dropping out of school. Why? Because it's boring.

"Compared to what!?"

We parents do react to bad grades. We might not react to activities. We might not react to friends. But, when that report card comes in and the grades have fallen, it is atom bomb time in the family. There is an emotional explosion because here is the first tangible proof that the alarm bell sounding within our brain is sounding for cause. There is now something factual telling us that we have reason to be concerned.

When I was in the drug treatment field, we could always count on our phone ringing off the hook during the two weeks after report cards came out. You could count on parents arriving, with a kid in one hand and a report card in the other. The parents would say, "I'm not sure, but I think we have a problem." They knew, they suspected because the school is our benchmark. Grades become our confirmation. A note from the teacher becomes our confirmation that something here is counterfeit.

But, then what do we do? Most of us do not immediately crank up the car and haul the kid to a drug treatment center to be tested for drugs. Most of us have a little talk with ourselves and our spouse: "We have got to crack down on Peggy. She's simply not applying herself."

So, we call the kid in for a big family conference. "You are hereby sentenced to study for 16 hours a day for the remainder of the school term. No Christmas, no holidays, no vacation till your grades are tops. Now, go up to your room and learn that algebra!"

Unfortunately, it is too late. The family becomes insane. One and all absolutely go bonkers. You sentence the kid to her room. Then, your spouse comes in and says, "Don't you think you're being a little bit too tough? If you had been tougher at the start of the school year, instead of being such a wimp..." That is the beginning of umpteen rounds of the Blame Game. It's your fault. It's the school's fault. It's his friend's fault. And on and on.

Each parent is so busy trying to affix blame on someone other than himself or herself, both fail to fix the real problem. The kid is sent to his or her room. Mom heads for the kitchen, the bedroom, the bathroom, or wherever she can close the door and separate herself from the situation. Dad goes to his sanctuary, which may be the garage or basement workshop where he can pound nails to release frustration. If he travels in his work, he will find excuses not to come home. I know I did. I well remember checking into a motel fifty miles from home just because I did not want to have to face my responsibilities.

You may be thinking: "But, all families do not have two parents living under the same roof. Like it or not, there are single moms and single dads." True. And, that is nothing new. There have always been, in some sense of the word, single parents.

In World War II, we took the vast majority of fathers in the country and shipped them overseas where many were killed. We took the mothers and sent them to the factories.

Still, we did not have a Toxic Culture. In earlier times, when people did not live long lives, disease, war, unsophisticated medical resources, and poor living conditions created single parent families.

I once read that during the Revolutionary War, as a percentage of population, there were more single parents in America than at any other time in history. Still, the Toxic Culture did not sweep the land... until recently.

Frankly, to some extent, being a true single parent is an advantage because you have no peer with whom to argue; you can be a benevolent dictator. On the other hand, often times, when there is a two-parent family, the child will play a game of "split 'em and get 'em". Every child knows that one "yes" makes up for a thousand "no's". So, in a two-parent household and in a divorce case, both parents must speak to the child with a unified front.

The trap divorced parents fall into is feeling guilty about subjecting the child to divorce. When they do, divorced parents often attempt to make it up to the child by trying to be the child's best buddy, not their father and mother. This action only makes matters worse because the last thing a child needs is a forty-year-old best buddy.

The Silent Sibling

When the mother and father of a toxic child, whether they are married or divorced, play round after round of the blame game, the younger siblings begin suspecting insanity runs in the family. They think you are blind to the truth because, nine times out of ten, the younger kids know exactly what is going on but cannot tell you. They cannot tell because, number one, if they do, they will have then "narced" on their big sister or brother; and number two, if they did tell, they know the parents will turn on them for not ratting sooner.

This split allegiance, no-win trap the younger kid is caught in, when part of a toxic family, can lead to something doubly tragic. The older child who is into the culture will often try to get the younger child or children involved. Why? To shut them up. To blackmail them. To give the parents, if they are caught, two or more targets, instead of one, on which they can take out their anger and frustration.

At this point, a family is in a terrible trap, and the toxic child is working hard on a bad self-image. Those activities, which started as a "party", have now moved inward and contaminated the whole family. What is left is a family that is at war with itself. It is a full-blown civil war that is taking place within the walls of what used to be considered a home. All have become the true victims of the American Toxic Culture.

Five Toxic Feelings

There are five feelings that you can experience when you walk into a Toxic home of a toxic person: fear, guilt, anger, depression, and loneliness. These feelings take up permanent residence because everybody in that family has now closed off. Instead of talking, instead of working it out, we run. We have our fights. We do not sit and talk about it face-to-face. I slam my door. You slam your door. They slam their doors. In short order, you have a house with every door in it closed; the people trapped there are sitting in little tiny compartments afraid, guilty, angry, depressed and very, very lonely.

Loneliness: that is the assassin; that is the killer. Horrible, overwhelming loneliness is the circumstance that causes kids to commit suicide or to think about committing suicide. They tell themselves over and over: "I'm a bad person. I'm an evil person. I'm a crazy person. I'm an insane person. After all, my family's bad, my school is bad, my friends are bad, and I have no dreams at all for the future. Why shouldn't I have a bad self-image? Why shouldn't I put an end to a bad thing here and now?"

Put any of us in that child's place and we would also have a bad self-image. Some people imply that today's youngsters are suffering from an epidemic of bad self-images. I really do not believe that all of a sudden we have produced a generation of kids who arrived on this planet with bad self-images. Every child is born with the most beautiful, wonderful self-image imaginable. Many, however, unlearn their positive self-image and replace it with a powerfully negative one. A negative self-image is the end result of the Toxic Culture of drugs, sex, and violence.

Four Behaviors That Demand Immediate Action

There are four behaviors that demand immediate action on your part. If you spot any of the four, immediately get help.

The first one is **runaway**. If your child runs away from home, get help at once. You are not involved in a game for amateurs and need competent, professional help.

The second **is theft** of property. Remember, I said that drugs consume two things: time and money. Theft is not limited to what might be stolen from a store, a neighbor, or a stranger. Theft also includes funds that, one way or another, come from your home. It might be your child's personal possessions that start to vanish, it might be money from the drawer where you dump your loose change. It might be cash lifted from your purse or wallet. It might be charges on that credit card your child is too young to have in the first place. The police should not have to call you to the station before you are faced with the problem of theft. Any form of theft whatsoever is solid reason to seek competent professional help.

The third behavior that cannot be ignored is any form of **physical violence**. Violence against you, your spouse, a sibling, other youngsters, a teacher, or anyone signals serious problems. Now, kids will fight; fighting is part of being a kid. However, violence for the sake of violence is what should sound the alarm bell. Explosive, violent rage wells from fear, guilt, depression, and loneliness. So, explosive, violent anger that is directed at you or your family cannot be dismissed as behavior that will pass.

The fourth behavior that demands immediate action is any **talk of suicide**. I do not mean action taken, an attempted suicide. That is an obvious situation that demands immediate intervention. Any talk about it is serious and must be viewed as a requirement for you to act. You may or may not be aware that there is a whole category of rock music out there that sells suicide as a solution. If you find your child gravitating towards music that rhapsodizes about ending it all, take action.

At any given point in life, we use the language at our disposal. A baby cannot talk; so, it cries and turns red in the face. That is the infant's way of communicating unhappiness or discomfort. Your teenager may have a way with words, but that does not mean she has the maturity and adult language skills to tell you in actual words that she is afraid of being swept up by the Toxic Culture.

We have to look to children's behaviors to know what is going on with them. It is virtually impossible for a child to walk up to a parent and say, "I'm afraid I'm getting caught up in something I can't handle; I'm using drugs, will you help me?"

So, behaviors become their form of communication, and as they did as babies, they act out their messages with behavior that causes you to help them. The point is words lie, but behavior never does. If you ignore the messages they send, the problem will only accelerate.

Competent Help

I assure you that the moment you suspect your child is being contaminated by the Toxic Culture is the moment to take action. The earlier you seek competent help, the better because the situation will not go away by itself. It is not a phase. Your child will not outgrow it. When I say "get competent help" I mean find some counselor, minister, drug treatment program, hospital, doctor, psychologist, psychiatrist, or physician, who truly understands the power of the Toxic Culture over kids. Furthermore, make certain that the counselor you turn to does not teach or use the concept of "responsible use." Ask point blank: "Do you teach or use the concept of responsible use?" If the answer is "sometimes" ... "yes" ... or "in certain cases," keep moving. Find somebody else.

There are toxic professionals, learned men and women who have bought into the Toxic Culture. In fact, they grew up in it and survived. You have to be cautious to whom you turn because some believe drug use is a normal, not a problem, and that some level of drug use is acceptable as a form of experimentation. They see it as a rite of passage, part of "normal development." "Normal", however, as I understand the word, means what the majority is doing, but what the majority may be doing is neither inherently wise nor healthy.

There is no such thing as responsible use of an illegal drug for a child. There is simply no such thing. Any tolerance on your part is taking part in introducing that drug into your child's brain. In my view, those who advocate so-called "responsible use" are saying to teach your child to hit himself or herself in the head with a chemical hammer responsibly. That is ridiculous. That is deranged. So, find a professional who knows about kids and drugs, has a track record in dealing successfully with the problem, and absolutely does not believe in the unfounded concept of "responsible use.

Awareness is your best friend. God gave you that alarm bell. Its purpose is to protect your child. Please have the wisdom, the love, and the courage to listen to it and respond... quickly and firmly. Ever heard of MammaRuski? No? You will meet her in a later chapter.

CHAPTER FIVE

REMEMBER THE DIFFERENCE

In our acrostic, PARENT, the R stands for Remember the Difference. While the difference between an adult and a child is easy to spot and understand, the difference between an adult and an adolescent is another matter. The problem is adolescents are really neither children nor adults. For me, this fact really hit home during a television interview, when a reporter asked me, "Isn't it a double standard for adults to drink and for kids not to be able to?"

I had probably faced that question a thousand times, but this was the first occasion on which I came up with an answer I really like. "Yes," I said, "it's a double standard ... because adolescence is a time of double standards."

Double Standards

There most certainly are double standards. Get over it. Consider the double standards built into adolescence, by custom and by law. Each is a sudden difference that becomes legal because of a birthday. Those listed below apply in most states.

AGE 12:

Movie ticket prices quadruple.

AGE 13:

Can attend movies rated PG-13.

AGE 14:

•Can hold a part-time job to pay for those movie tickets.

•The age of sexual consent. (Previous sexual activity of any kind is statutory rape.)

•Marriage without parental consent is permissible.

Children of divorced parents can demand final say, concerning with whom they live.

AGE 15:

*Can receive learner's permit to drive a car, when accompanied by an adult.

AGE 16:

•Can receive a drivers license.

•Move from junior high to high school.

•Can quit school.

AGE 17:

•Can attend a movie rated NC-17

•Can attend R-rated movies, if accompanied by a parent.

•Moves from the juvenile justice system to the adult justice system.

AGE 18:

•Can purchase cigarettes.

•Can gamble.

•Can attend movies rated R and NC-17 without being accompanied by a parent.

•Can sign a contract and be held responsible for living up to its terms.

•Males must register for the draft.

•Can vote.

AGE 21:

•   Can purchase alcoholic beverages.

My point in calling attention to all of the above is not to analyze the logic in some of the laws and our generally-held customs; my point is to show we do not suddenly create an adult on the twenty-first birthday. We create an adult over about a twenty-one year period, turning over responsibility to young people as we assume they can handle it. We do this both in society and in the family.

Family, Inc.

In certain ways, a family is like a corporation, one in which the parents initially hold all the voting "stock." At an early age, a child is given one share of stock, just enough to voice an opinion. In other words, the child can say she does not want to eat her green beans or go to bed at the appointed time; however, her one share of voting stock is automatically out-voted by a parent. As the years pass, the child is given more and more stock. In theory, we dole it out at intervals determined by the child having proven, through his actions, that he is worthy of authority and wants to assume responsibility for his actions.

While the child may think he or she is ready to assume responsibility, as well as authority, the relationship between authority and responsibility in the family is little different from in the military and the business world. All military institutions and business schools teach that you, the person in charge, may delegate authority; however, you can never delegate sole responsibility. You remain responsible for the actions of anyone under your supervision. If you give your child the authority to drive your car and she wrecks it, you remain financially responsible. The same thing is true if your child commits vandalism or any other offense; you, the parent, remain legally and ethically responsible. So, when your child abuses any authority granted by you, that authority should be withdrawn.

Through painful trial and error, society has determined the earliest, the minimum age at which most adolescents can handle particular responsibilities. Obviously, some of these items I have listed are legal rights, such as voting and signing a contract. But, by law and by custom, most decisions are left to the discretion of parents.

For example, while it is probable that your child can handle the various responsibilities listed at the legal age, it is your right and responsibility, as a parent, to decide when your child is old enough to exercise most of these various freedoms and privileges. Just because the law makes provisions for 16-year-olds to drive does not mean that your child has a Constitutional right to drive at 16 — much less deserves to be given a car. It only means age 16 is the earliest that you can allow your child to test for a license to drive. At 16, your child may or may not be capable of handling a four thousand pound piece of machinery in multiple lanes of traffic that are traveling at 70 miles an hour. That decision is yours.

Likewise, the law concerning attending movies rated NC-17 merely sets age 18 as the earliest point in time when you can allow your child to attend. As long as the child lives under your roof, the above are decisions you should make. For example, you have the responsibility to say a child living under your roof cannot smoke at the legal age for purchasing tobacco products. It is your house, not the child's; so, you set the rules.

Freedom and Trust

One of the drives of adolescents is a hunger for freedom. Recalling what Maslow taught us, we know the desire for freedom, the ability to do one's own thing, is basic to human nature and certainly natural for an emerging adult. Our children express this yearning for freedom in terms of trust. When we disallow something, we hear, "You don't trust me."

We have become convinced by psycobabble and popular culture that we should automatically trust children. Nothing is further from the truth. By definition, a child is someone not yet ready to be fully trusted. Children are not inherently evil; they are, however, inherently immature and inherently human. This is why we have separate courts, separate laws, and separate regulations that cover hiring of children, curfews, and the treatment they receive when they break the law. These institutions and laws are in place because it is our duty as parents and as a society to protect children from their own stupidity.

In order to properly protect our children, we must have among our parenting tools some means of determining when each child is worthy of various forms and degrees of trust. We cannot base trust on what a child says; words can lie. I am a big fan of Judge Judy who says that "if a kids lips are moving, they are lying". Also, to quote the Judge again, "when a teenager gets out of bed in the morning, they begin to lie."

We must base trust on what a child does, on his or her actions because actions never lie. So, the parenting tool I suggest involves use of a three-filter system. The first filter is labeled Dependability, the second Responsibility, and the third

Accountability. If their actions pass all three filters, we can feel confident in increasing our level of trust.

Dependability, Responsibility, and Accountability are words we tend to toss around without considering what they really mean. So, let us divide each word and inspect its parts.

Depend ... ability means the ability to depend on someone or something. In other words, a dependable person is one who will do what he says he will do because a dependable person keeps his word. He tells the truth. He delivers on his promise. This does not mean that all people and all things that are dependable are equal. For example, both a Honda Accord and a Mercedes 390 SL are dependable automobiles. They are dependable because they live up to their promise. The Honda Accord does not promise 150 miles an hour on the Autobahn and ultimate luxury; it merely promises to start and get you around town.

So, being dependable is doing what you say you will do; it is keeping one's word, whether the promise made is small or great. All of us like to work with, be friends with, and be in a family with people who keep their word. So, we ask ourselves, has our child reached the point he can be relied upon to be Dependable? Does he simply keep his word?

Assuming a child has matured to the point her actions prove she is dependable, someone who keeps her word, we move to the second filter, Responsibility. When we break this word apart, we have responsible and ability: able to respond appropriately by doing what one needs to do, instead of what one wants to do. There are times when I do not want to go to work. Nonetheless, I have learned, as an adult, that I need to go to work, in spite of the fact that I sometimes would prefer not to do. It takes responsibility to override the desire to goof off, to seek amusement, to ignore obligations. So, we ask ourselves, has our child reached the point she can be relied upon to be responsible and do what needs to be done, rather than what the child wants to do?

If the child's actions pass this second filter, we move on to Accountability, which is also a simple concept. Broken apart, we have the words accountable and responsible, the ability to make an accounting. That means you take ownership of your actions. You no longer try blaming your friend or your sister, your coach or teacher. You did it; so, you own the results of your actions.

When a child's actions pass the tests of all three filters of Dependability, Responsibility, and Accountability you can assume he or she is worthy of your trust.

Building Trust

Let's further examine that issue of Trust, especially since it is a word our children use a lot. When we say "no" to something they want permission to do, we hear: "You don't trust me." As we have established, not trusting your child merely means you do not yet see the signs of maturity and character development that generate trust on your part. The next time your child complains about your lack of trust, first recognize that when your child uses the word "trust" she is really saying she wants to cut a deal with you; so, cut one — but only on your terms. First, in effect, say to them, if you give me Dependability, Responsibility, and Accountability, I will give you Trust. If you do not, I will not give you Trust. That's the deal. Second, recognize the situation as a golden opportunity to explain to your child that you are eager to be able to trust her.

Let me make a major point here. **Trust is never given; it is always earned.** Tell your child the truth; when she earns your trust through actions that show maturity (i.e. Dependability,

Responsibility, and Accountability), you will gladly deliver all the trust imaginable. She or he must be lead to understand that the real world does not cut deals, where trust is concerned. Trust is always earned through appropriate performance. Is the child worthy of your trust? Furthermore, you would be shirking your responsibility if you failed to require your child to exhibit actions that generate trust. Forget what I just said! It would be stupid to do so!

For example, suppose tomorrow you go to work at a bank. You walk into the office of that bank's president and say, "Hi, I'm here to be Chairman of the Board." That bank president is going to look at you as if you are some kind of kook because that is not how real life in a bank operates. They start by putting you in charge of the pennies, the nickels, and the dimes. If you do a good job with the small change, in a month or two, they give you the quarters and the dollar bills. If you do a good job with those, they promote you to fives, tens, and twenties. If you do a great job with them, they entrust you with the hundreds and the thousands. If you do a wonderful job with them, they entrust you with the vault. If you do a spectacular job with the vault, they make you Executive Vice President ... Head of the Loan Department ... President of the Bank ... Chairman of the Board. But, no one automatically gives you trust, great responsibility and the titles that accompany outstanding performance. You, like every Chairman of the Board before you, earn every bit of it. So, I say we must raise our kids to function in the real world where trust is acquired in only one way: it is earned.

When you reach the point where your child has earned your trust, remember that trust does not rule out common sense. While your child may be trustworthy, the world he or she lives in is not. Therefore, trusting does not mean that your child should be allowed to drive 300 miles to a rock concert and get home at four in the morning simply because he or she is dependable, responsible, and accountable enough to drive to the market for a gallon of milk. Even though a sixteen-year-old can legally make the trip to the rock concert, he or she does not yet qualify for the privilege or the late hours because such things are age inappropriate. It still remains your responsibility to protect your child from a very untrustworthy world.

Education and Training

Next, consider from what source your child should learn Dependability, Responsibility, and Accountability, the elements that generate Trust. At first, it might sound as if it is the school's job. There was a time when I thought that way.

When my daughter got into drugs, the first place I went was the school principal's office. I was furious, and I blistered him up one side and down the other. "Why aren't you doing a better job running this school? My daughter got into trouble with drugs!"

He was very kind and very courteous as he showed me the front door. Later, I went back and apologized to him. And, I should have. Here is why.

Remember, in the introduction of the book I said, if the 60 minutes marked on a clock's face represent a person's life from birth until age 18, only 5.6 minutes of that time is spent in school. That's barely enough time to educate a child.

Nonetheless, when we saw our children did not drive well, we told the schools to teach drivers Ed. When we realized our children were getting into drugs, we told the schools to introduce drug education programs. As our children became involved in pregnancies, we said the school should teach them sex education. When our children got into fights with one another, we said introduce conflict resolution in our schools. Now that our children are becoming involved with guns, some people are advocating gun safety classes in our schools.

You may say, "Well, these are matters where the church should come in." But, when we take another look at that clock, we see that the child who goes to church, to synagogue, to a youth group, or to whatever spiritually and morally based organization you prefer is in that environment for a very short time.

Even if your child regularly attends all worship services and Vacation Bible School or other religious instruction classes, only .7 minutes of the time on that clock face are spent in a structured religious environment. So, if you add the .7 minutes of religious influence with the 5.6 minutes of school influence, that means a grand total of just 6.3 "minutes" out of a child's 60 minutes of youth is influenced by the institutions of religious and educational instruction. The rest of the time, the vast majority of the time, the child is your responsibility.

Here is the point I want to make with this. We have increasingly taken areas of training (i.e., behavior) and redefined them as education (i.e., knowledge), but it is not working. It is not working because we have not increased the length of the school day or the time children are in a structured religious environment.

Furthermore, I am not certain that would be the appropriate action because the primary place and time for acquiring morals, values, and appropriate behavior patterns is the third time slot: time under parental supervision.

We become confused on this issue by failing to realize that knowledge and training are not synonymous. When I stormed into the principal's office, I had forgotten an important fact: the purpose of education is to impart knowledge; the purpose of training is to teach behavior.

We started out that way and told the schools: "You give them knowledge, we'll handle their behavior." Then, as the years progressed, we started holding the schools more and more accountable for our job. Not that the schools cannot help in all these areas; it can if there is time left after teaching and testing for knowledge of language, literature, math, science, and history.

In spite of the time allocation problems, at least in one beyond-the-call-of-duty area, the schools have done an excellent job. On the school property, the war on drugs has been won. We now have virtually drug-free schools. What we do not have are drug-free kids.

The organization known as PRIDE , Parent's Resource Institute and Drug Education (pridesurveys.com), surveyed kids in school. The adolescents were asked many questions about drug and alcohol use, questions concerning what drugs they used, what form of alcohol they consumed, at what age did use begin? An amazing about of information was gathered, and out of PRIDE's findings, the most significant information learned, in my opinion, was the answers to these questions: When do you use? and Where do you use?

Concerning When do you use?, their findings show a tiny percentage of kids use before school; however, an even lesser percentage of kids use during school. But, the percentages start to grow when you reach the after-school hours, the unsupervised time between the end of the school day and the return of parents to the home. The numbers increase at night and soar during weekends. Saturday night is the time when the majority of America's young drug users and drinkers indulge.

In answer to the question, Where do you use?, a substantial number said they use at home. In many cases, their source is the family medicine cabinet or liquor cabinet. At a friend's house was another frequent answer. In a car, while cruising — especially on Saturday nights — had the highest numbers, followed closely by a lovers' lane or some other spot where the community agrees to leave teens alone. Every town has such a place.

The least used location is the school. Virtually no one uses at school. They may deal at school. They may possess at school. They may plan the party at school. But, in today's world, if kids are going to use, they leave that school property to do it. The is true for drinking, having sex, and becoming involved in violence. At the time I am writing this book, parents are highly anxious about their children being exposed to violence during school hours. But, the same parents do not seem overly concerned about the greater possibility of there being a gun at the shopping mall or the party their children attend on Saturday night.

All parents need to realize that the school property has become the most drug-free, alcohol-free, violence-free piece of real estate within their communities. The times when these children are using drugs, drinking, having sex, and being exposed to violence are almost always when we parents are in charge. So, that tells us the schools are doing a far better job than we parents. That is good reason to go to your school and, instead of berating the principal as I did, give the principal a hug — at least a hearty "thank-you." Both are well deserved. Let your principal know that you understand the school's job is to educate, while your job, as a parent, is to supply the training.

A Training Model

In my seminars, when the subject of training is discussed and the consequences of behavior is mentioned, I find we parents tend to think first of negative behavior, rather than positive behavior. Furthermore, we tend to think in terms of punishment, rather than reward. There should be consequences for both good behavior and for bad.

First, let us focus on the consequences of positive behavior. When I think of expert training, I think of Sea World and its star attraction, Shamu, the whale. That whale is not only educated, he is beautifully trained. At a signal, Shamu rises out of the water, jumps through a hoop, and goes back into the water. To train him to perform the feat, a hoop was introduced into his environment and placed upright near the bottom of the tank. Then, the trainers simply watched. They did not yell at the whale when he failed to swim through the loop, nor did they punish him.

Instead, they waited until Shamu accidentally swam through the hoop. The moment he did, a bell was rung, and they gave him a fish. By accident, he repeated the act. When he did, again the bell rang and dinner was served. In short order, the whale got the message: swim through the hoop, ring a bell, and get a fish.

Over time, they raised the hoop higher and higher. Soon the whale was leaping out of the water in order to sail through the hoop, knowing when he did, the bell would sound and he would be rewarded.

That is positive reinforcement in its purest form. The whale's trainers do not criticize or punish Shamu when he fails to perform in the way they want him to perform. Instead, they stay on the lookout for positive behavior and reward him each time it occurs.

There are books about highly successful companies that operate on the principle called "Catch Someone Doing Something Right." It is the same approach used at Sea World to train Shamu. In these companies, management's job is to spot desirable performance. When they see it happening, they lay on the praise and the reward. Does it work? You bet it does!

—

86

Productivity and quality in those companies out-distance the competition simply because positive reinforcement works. It works on whales, it works in the business world, and it works with little kids and with adolescents.

One survey that I read said, on average, a parent spends 15 minutes a day in meaningful conversation with his or her children. Thirteen of that 15 minutes are spent criticizing what the children do. I suggest you can double the power of your parenting by spending 15 minutes a day praising your children for what they do absolutely right by accident.

Sometimes kids, like adults, backslide. When they do, they lose our trust. What should happen then? Do we punish them? As I understand the word "punish", I believe it is not the appropriate action. Punishment is the act of getting even. I suggest that a better approach is allowing teenagers to reap the consequences of their actions. When consequences come into play, you are actually teaching that child. So, one of the problems that we parents have is determining how we should realistically set consequences for our children's actions.

One way to approach the issue of consequences is from the standpoint of your child's wants and your child's needs. When we, as adults, make that list, we focus on many of the needs that Maslow identified: clothing, food, recognition, security, and intimacy. None of these things should ever be denied. Saying, "If you don't do as I say, I won't love you," is the very worst thing you can do.

Your child may not have a clear understanding of the difference between a want and a need. A friend of mine told me about his daughter coming to him, saying she just had to have a pair of designer jeans. When he learned the price of the jeans — and it was a steep one — he told her, "Look, I am obligated by law to

cover your rear end. I am not, however, obligated to decorate it."
In other words, while clothing is a need, decoration is not.
Decoration goes on the list of wants.

The list of a teenager's wants also includes money,
entertainment, use of a car, use of the telephone, television,
freedom, music, and sports. Your child may have additional
wants, however, for sake of example, we will work with these
virtually universal ones, and we will link these wants with
consequences.

When you do make the link, when you make it possible for them
to realize their reasonable wants through correct behavior, they
become the controller of their fate; they become the person who
determines consequences.

It is no longer vindictive punishment; it is reward for doing
things right or denial for doing things that are not appropriate.
They can earn or deny themselves the things they deeply want by
their behavior. You link a consequence to their behavior when
they earn their wants; you teach them — not punished them.

Link Behavior and Consequences

Linking behavior with the appropriate consequence may take
some thought on your part. For example, suppose your child
misses curfew by half an hour. What is a want you can withdraw
to teach a lesson? What is a way you can link the violation with
the consequences? Just because your child virtually lives to
watch a particular TV program, denying her or him the privilege
of watching it is not the right choice because watching TV had
nothing to do with the violation. Instead, I suggest linking the
violation with curfew time by saying, "Since you missed curfew
by 30 minutes, curfew moves up 30 minutes; instead of having to
be home by eleven, you will have to be home by ten-thirty until I

am convinced you understand the importance of respecting a curfew." On the other hand, if the child fails to do his homework or chores because he is living in front of the TV, limit his television time.

Both of the above examples tie the consequence to the offense. And, when the link is made, you are teaching, not punishing. Love is not withheld. Food, shelter, security, and recognition are not withheld. All the true needs are still filled.

I will admit that, when we are worried, concerned, and emotionally upset by inappropriate behavior, it may not be the best time to decide what the consequences of a violation should be. What we forget, as parents, is that we have not signed an agreement with our children that states we will, on the spot, announce the consequences of future violations. A waiting period can do more than give you time to think the situation through in a level-headed manner. That is the usual approach in our court system. Judges give themselves a period of time to study the matter and make certain their decision is wise, appropriate, and prudent.

Use of the waiting period was certainly my mother's approach. She would never act quickly. When I did something wrong, she would think about the consequence for a day. For me, it became a day of sheer agony. When her pronouncement came, I was falling-down grateful to face the consequences of my actions.

While my mother customarily took a day, there is no rule or contract between you and your child that requires you to act even that quickly. Take your time. Make certain the consequence is appropriate to the situation. If you run out of ideas, consult a friend who is not emotionally tied in knots over the situation, as you are. Taking your time will make a difference in the quality of your training and the value your child receives from it. On the other hand, if your aim is to punish, rather than to train, you might as well go ahead and inflict your chosen punishment because punishment seldom generates positive results, no matter the time factor involved.

In choosing a consequence for negative behavior, far too many of us automatically ground a teenager for a period of time, as if it were some suitable-for-all-offenses action. I recommend thinking long and hard before grounding a child for any length of time because grounding frequently becomes unenforceable. If you ground your child for a month, you are grounding yourself for the same period of time. Unless you are different from most of us, you reach a point where you find enforcing the grounding is so difficult and time-consuming that you weaken and reduce the "sentence", which teaches your child that you cannot live up to your own rules and regulations.

The point I want to make is our goal as parents is not to punish, it is not to inflict pain; instead, it is to teach the child that privileges are earned. When you teach the value of appropriate behavior through rewards and consequences, you are really preparing your child for the very real world of adulthood.

Neither positive nor negative consequences should be a surprise to a child. Children should be made aware that each time additional freedom and trust are doled out, there will be consequences because you hold them responsible for their actions.

I know of quite a few parents who are dealing, in creative and constructive ways, with the challenge of doling out trust and the privileges that accompany trust. For example, when one dad's son got his driver's license, the dad hugged and congratulated his boy, saying: "Son, I'm so proud of you for being 16. Now, I want to show you a letter I've written to the State Department of

Motor Vehicles. If I ever catch you driving recklessly, this letter revokes your license. Now, I'm not going to mail this letter; I'm going to put it right here in my desk. But, I make you this promise: if you choose to use and ignore the law, I'm sending the letter. Whether I send it or not is your choice."

Few parents know that in most states, the power to cancel their child's driver's license is theirs. This is a very persuasive and useful parenting tool.

Another parent I met, during one of my seminars, told me she had a written contract with her daughter about the consequences of drinking or using drugs. I like the contract idea. It is not punishment. It clearly establishes that the outcome is the young person's responsibility because the authority is being turned over to the child. If the teenager violates the contract, her violation determines the consequences.

That is what we do with adults, is it not? We say, it is an adult's choice to do or not do certain things; however, if the adult violates the rules, privileges and rights are forfeited.

I know another parent who gave his son extraordinary opportunities: the best schools, extensive world travel, exposure to sports and the arts. But, from the time the boy could say, the word "car", his dad made it clear that the great driving lesson his son would receive was the experience of earning the money to pay for that first automobile. The result of the parent taking that stand is a young man who drives the car he bought as if it were an egg.

During the developing years, we must remember the differences between the child, the adolescent, and the adult. There are continual changes that reconstruct those differences in rapid fashion. We, as the adults, have to stay consciously aware of the differences and the changes in order to shepherd our offspring safely to the status of trustworthy adulthood. That is part of the job description of a parent.

CHAPTER SIX

EXPECT AND INSPECT

The E in our acrostic, PARENT, stands for Expect and Inspect. In this chapter, our initial focus is on the importance of your family belief system and what you expect from your child as a human being. After correctly establishing our expectations, we will shift focus to the importance of inspecting your family belief system, yourself, and your loved ones, in order to make sure your beliefs are being upheld.

Expect Versus Inspect

When my Latin teacher was explaining how to break words into their basic components, one of the root words that burned into my brain was "spectare", which means to "see" or to "look". It is the root of many of our words, such as spectacles, specter, and spectator. It is also the root of expect and inspect. To create expect, the prefix ex, which means "out," is added; so, expect means to look out. Inspect is the other side of the coin. By adding the prefix in, we create a word that means to look within. To live up to our duty as parents, we must first set expectations. Then, second, we must inspect to see if our expectations are being realized.

One of the challenges parents have in this age of high achievers is to set expectations that are both desirable and realistic. In reality, children at all levels are not going to always look good and perform well. For example, it comes as a disappointment and a shock to parents of high intellect when they discover they have a child of average intellect. Likewise, it can be a disappointment to an exceptional athlete to discover his or her child did not inherit equal or greater physical abilities. Yet, these same children may have gifts, talents, and abilities that their parents do not possess.

Recently, I broached this subject with a group of parents whose children are enrolled in a private school. "You are all high achievers," I told the parents. "If your children have God-given skills that are different from yours, that fact does not make them better or worse; it only means they are different." When I said this, the school's headmaster stood up and applauded. He knows how important it is for us to value the average performer, as well as the super achiever. Face it, many of us are average.

Average Really Is Normal

This country was built by average people. Average athletes. Average intellectual performers. By definition, most of us are average, and few of us are super stars. Nonetheless, "average people" can do extraordinary things. I can show you people who were academically well below average during their school years, but today they have made fortunes through their special abilities. One of the reasons is we often do not value in children the talents and abilities that we value in adults. In children, for example, we call the ability to shift from one subject to another very quickly attention deficit disorder and usually medicate those children so that they will be unobtrusive in an academic environment. That same ability to shift rapidly from one subject to another, however, is highly valued when it is found in the CEO of a company.

On the heels of the above statements, I want to quickly tell you that financial success is not the only worthy goal in life. Our expectations must first focus on character, then on the maximization of abilities. When we set expectations beyond those that have to do with character, we must keep our expectations realistic. If we do not, we cripple the child's sense of confidence, and without confidence, little can be accomplished.

You may want your child to throw a 95 mile an hour fast ball, but the first 10,000 thrown will probably be at 30 miles an hour ... then inch up to 35 ... then to 40. It is fine, as time passes, to raise the bar of your expectations to a new and achievable goal, one that is based on a combination of ability and performance. This applies academically, as well. If your child comes home with a D in math, do not automatically devalue that D. Your child may have worked harder for the D than another child had to work for an A.

So, recognize and celebrate effort, first and foremost. This does not call for dumbing down the standards; it calls for personalizing the standards and shoring up confidence.

Confidence is the solid step that can take a person up to the next achievable level. Instead of setting standards based on our own personal strengths, we must play to the child's strengths. Often playing to a child's strengths is more a matter of simply getting out of the way and applauding accomplishment. A basketball coach who agrees with that approach once told me, "The talent of a Michael Jordan is not taught; it is latent at birth. What a good coach does is simply protect and encourage natural ability."

So, what that coach is advocating is exactly what we discovered was the secret used to train Shamu the whale to do extraordinary things: create conditions that involve achievable goals, and reward desired action that is performed through both effort and accident. When you stand ready to recognize and reward all worthy achievement, your child wants to excel.

One of the best ways of determining the achievement standards that are appropriate for your child to take is through professionally administered aptitude testing. I am not referring to intelligence tests; I am talking about tests that reveal the natural gifts, talents, and abilities that are within your child and likely lying dormant.

A call to your school should connect you with a testing service. The costs are reasonable, and the results can be invaluable. I even suggest you have your child tested at least every other year. We did this for our second child, Julie. The tests clearly revealed that physics and mathematics were not her strong suites, but the tests did show the areas in which she could excel. We think it is one of the best things we ever did for her… she does too.

Eleven Ways to Raise a Toxic Child

When a child is not advancing at the speed we would prefer, it is a great temptation to jump in and act on their behalf. That is not a direction in which we parents should travel. To get where we need to go, we need to understand where we do not want to go. So, I offer the following list of sure-fire ways to raise a toxic child. Do these things, play these roles and, at some point in time, you will end up trying to salvage your child's life from the ravages of drugs, sexual promiscuity, violence, or any combination of the three.

The first way is to become your child's **Lawyer**. Any time there is the slightest bit of criticism of your child, from a school teacher or from a counselor or from the principal, march down to the school and present your child's defense. Present their case. Make the counter argument. Hardly a day goes by without parents striding into the school with ears closed to information they need. They are not there to listen and learn what is going on with their children; they are there to defend.

The second role that you can play for your child is that of **Banker**. Make it a simple, routine process for your child to treat you as if you are a teller at their bank. "Mom, may I have $20?" "Why sure, darling, here it is." That is the real world. That is how it happens. The child simply asks for money and gets it.

The third role you can assume is that of your child's **Insurance** Company. Create a situation that is the same as your child's having a policy with a bottomless funding mechanism. When there is trouble, you pay the price. She gets the ticket; you go to court. You show up and represent her. In that way, you let your child know, no matter what she does, she has the full resources of your family behind her every activity.

The fourth role you can assume is that of your child's **Agent**. Represent him; negotiate the best deals in life for them. The kid is not ready to play varsity football, but you go to the coach and say, "Hey, coach, we've got an up-and-coming super star here. All this kid needs is a little playing time." Your daughter is not ready to be the head cheerleader, but because of your own personal politics you can work it out so that she gets the position. When you do, you teach your child she or he is of no value, that it really takes you to make things happen for them.

The fifth role you can assume for your children is **Mechanic**. Fix for her whatever she breaks. When she comes home after having a bad day, rather than letting her figure out what went wrong and how to deal with it like healthy responsible people do, you give her the instant solution. "Darling, here's what you do. You say this, you go here. I'll make this phone call and fix it all up." I was Mr. Fix It. I could fix any problem. Any time a problem came along, my girls knew I would fix it. No problem was too big to for Super Dad. I know better now.

You can also assume the role of **Butler.** You can prepare your child for life in a luxury hotel. After all, he is going to be successful one day; he is going to make a lot of money one day and will surely be living in spas and mansions. So, make the beds for him. Clean up his room for him. Have the meals ready on time. Heaven forbid that dinner should not be ready when he shows up! If you're going to prepare a child for life in the lap of luxury, you may as well start very, very young.

Here is another role you can assume: be your child's **Fairy God Mother**. Wave your wand and make it happen. Take a shrinking family checking account and instantly fix whatever needs a cash infusion. "Whatever you want, darling, you don't have to wait for it." Teach her to get instant gratification from life. Do not let her earn it. Do not let her work for it. Do not let her wait for it. In your house it is Christmas every day.

Definitely be your child's **Doormat**. Let him take out his frustrations on you. He gets upset. He gets angry. So, let him just dump all over you. You may feel that doing so teaches him humility by example. It does not. It does, however, teach your child to use people and take advantage of their affection.

By all means be your child's **Apologist**. Give her a good excuse for everything that comes along. Whatever your daughter does, give her a good excuse for it. "Well, sweetheart, it's not really your fault; it's Dad's fault." When you daughter brings home a D on a test, accept the blame. Make it so that she can explain to the teacher that she would have loved to have made a B on that algebra test, but her parents play the television so loud at night, she simply cannot concentrate on homework.

Be your child's **Administrative Assistant**. Serve as secretary. For example, grades are extremely important; without good grades, your children can not get into a good college. So, do your part toward assuring your child impressive transcripts. Do not let him do that project alone. Do not let him make that good, honest C with character. No. Apply your adult skills and be sure your kid gets an A. When you do, you will find your child is quite willing to step aside and let you earn A's. He knows that is not his A. He knows who earned it, and he knows who did not earn it.

And finally, while you are busy, busy, busy being Lawyer, Banker, Insurance Company, Agent, Mechanic, Butler, Fairy Godmother, Doormat, Apologist, and Administrative Assistant for your child, also **fail to teach a family belief system**. Definitely take the approach that says: "I'm going to let my children wait until they're 21 and decide for themselves." By doing all these things, you can assure that, at some point, your child will become engulfed in the Toxic Culture.

Teaching A Belief System

I watch it happen all the time. Children drift toward toxic attractions because parents are allowing children to wait until they are 21 to decide some of the most important issues of life. But, the children are not waiting; they are deciding at 12, 13, 14, and 15, based on someone else's advice. Having a belief system is terribly important in our lives. Our belief system lets us know when we are right and when we are wrong. You can call it a conscience.

You may call it whatever you want to call it, but if I teach my child a belief system, that child has three options when dealing with the family belief system. We will explore those options in a moment. First, let's fix an image in our minds. Think of that belief system as a line in the dirt, one that is clearly drawn and retraced frequently to keep it plainly visible.

In Government, the line is called a Law or Regulation. In Business, it is a Policy or Precedure. In the Family, it is a Rule.

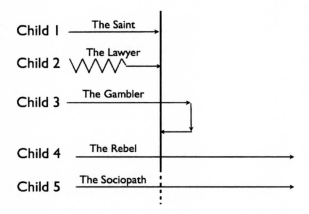

When that line exists and is well understood by the child, the child has five five choices.

Child One: the child can go up to the limits of the belief and, because that belief system is in place, she does not go past it; he does not violate his conscience. The child says, "Uh-oh, I can't go beyond this point; I can't do that. I would love to do some things with you, but I can't do that." I call this child The Saint". You only get one of these.

Child Two: Complains, argues, negotiates, debates but when push comes to shove, obeys the rule. This child is The Lawyer. I am like that at Income Tax time. After weeks of complaining and procrastinating, I will be at the Post Office at midnight on April 15th.

Child Three: Pushes the limit, crosses the line, but worries about getting caught, turns around and comes back to the line. The best example of this has to do with the speed limit. Many folks believe in their heart that Law Enforcement will "give you" ten miles above the speed limit on the Interstates. They carefully set their cruise control at that limit. When they see what just might be a Police Cruiser coming their way, they tap their brake pedal and coast below the limit. This is simply the American way. To some extent, we are a nation of Gamblers.

Child Four: The Rebel knows right from wrong but chooses to do wrong. This is an immoral person. Their eventual destination is prison, the emergency room, the cemetery, or a rehabilitation center.

Child Five: The Sociopath has no line at all. They are simply "amoral." This is a very scary person. We are saying that this child has "no moral compass", "no sense of right and wrong", "no conscience". Beware these kids... and their parents.

What I have learned from working with teens in trouble is a child who has been denied careful teaching of a worthy family belief system is very difficult to help, to ever be rehabilitated. Rehabilitation is bringing a person back to where they ought to be. If there is no worthy belief system to which the child can return, he has nowhere to go. A child, however, who falls into our second category, one who has violated the limits of the family belief system and returned at least once, is a child who can be rehabilitated. She has a point to which she can return. He can be helped. And, these children can help themselves. The mere fact that we are concerned about rehabilitation says the child has gone past something — but is being helped to return to a norm, to return to a standard.

If you have never taught your child a belief system, you will never know when the child has strayed too far until it is obvious he or she has been swept away by the Toxic Culture. You will not know because you, just like your child, will have no guideposts or references for meaningful measurement and evaluation. So, knowing what to look for is terribly, terribly important.

Sad to say, the family with morals has become almost outdated. Morals have been branded as "out of style." But, we are paying a price for the lack of them. When you wipe out belief, when you do not stand up for a set of well-defined beliefs, the family does not necessarily become immoral; however, it does become amoral. The family becomes amoral because it stands for nothing. Anything goes. If you make the decision that anything goes in your family, then you had better be prepared to pay the price for that "anything" that does go.

I have heard some try to defend their "amoral, anything-goes" approach as "freedom."

It is not freedom; it is license. The jails are full of these folks. Nowhere in this country have we ever believed that license and freedom went hand-in-hand.

Think about it. You have a license to drive. The next time you get into your car, you could drive onto an interstate and go anywhere in this nation. No signal light will stop you. As long as you stay in the lanes and within the speed limit, you can go till you run out of gas. But, if you make the decision that you want to do it your way, speed up to 100 miles per hour and take off cross country, you will either be arrested or get killed.

I suggest to you that one of the reasons we have so many kids getting killed today is we are allowing them, at very young ages, to make their own decisions about the family belief system. That is a decision they are too young and too inexperienced to make.

If You Stand For Nothing, You Will Fall For Anything.

If you think I am making too much of the need for a family belief system, pick any family or any organization you respect and take a hard look at it. Pick the Rotary Club, pick Kiwanis, pick a cheerleader group, pick a church, pick an environmental group, and pick any organization you truly respect. It will have a belief system.

We have a belief system in America. It is called the Constitution of the United States, and our Constitution determines what an American is. We believe in it; so, when we start to feel something is wrong, we appeal to our national belief system. We say the thing that is wrong is unconstitutional. We say it because we hold that our belief system has been violated.

A belief system defines a group's identity and determines why that group exists. That belief system is the basis for group pride. I do not mean pride in the negative sense; I mean pride in the sense of belonging, that critical need that Maslow identified.

I had the pleasure and honor of serving as our local ROTARY Club's President for a year. ROTARY has a Four Way Test that summarizes the Club's Belief System:

> Is It The Truth?

> Is It Fair To All Concerned?

> Will It Build Goodwill And Better Friendships?

> Is It Beneficial To All Concerned?

When I was in Emory University, we had a strictly enforced Honor Code:

"I will neither lie nor cheat nor steal nor tolerate those that do."

As an Officer in the US Air Force, we had an Honor Code:

"I will neither lie nor cheat nor steal nor tolerate those that do."

When I was a Boy Scout (Eagle... thank you very much!), we had a belief system in the form of The Scout Oath:

"On My Honor I Will Do My Best To Do My Duty To God And My Country And To Obey The Scout Law. To Help Other People At All Times And To Keep Myself Physically Strong, Mentally Awake, And Morally Straight."

Get the point?

One other thing here. The belief system must be short, frequently stated, publically acknowleged and memorable... maybe even memorized. God only gave ten commandments... only ten commandments... only ten.

I had a good friend, a Reporter, who said one day that a good newspaper editor would have boiled The Ten Commandments down to one word... DON"T!

Pride in belonging can lead in either desirable or undesirable directions. Pride in belonging is the appeal of gangs to the young. We can learn much from gangs. We can learn what they offer that we are failing to provide. No matter how repulsive you and I may find gangs, there is no denying that gangs have a belief system, and their members find a place where they are valued, rules and regulations that create a sense of order. In a gang, there is leadership, challenge, the distinction of being part of a select group, and the ability to excel — even if it means excelling in all the wrong things.

We want to belong to something significant. Kids may think: "This so-called family I belong to has no beliefs attached to it." That is the child who looks to gangs and the Toxic Culture for guidance. On the other hand, a child may be part of a family that has a firmly entrenched belief system that does not appeal to the child. They may think your belief system is outdated, peculiar, or insignificant. Even so, because the family takes a stand, the child — despite his frustrations — understands that the family belief system makes his or her family unique.

Kids like unique families. However, they will never tell you that. They will never walk up to you and confess: "Dad, this is a wonderful family because we have these guidelines." But, let me assure you, they will tell their friends that. They will tell their closest buddy. Likely you are thinking: "I don't believe that's the case." But, it is.

I do not want to appear holier than thou about belief systems. The Oliver family's belief system and making it thoroughly understood came as a result of some awfully tragic circumstances. We had to develop and promote ours, or we were going to die. I wish I could tell you we promoted our belief system earlier than we did. However, that is not the case. Nonetheless, once it was in place, promoted, and practiced, the day came when a friend of my youngest daughter sat on the floor of our den, teared up, and said, "I'd love to belong to a family like this."

I consider that one of the greatest compliments I have ever had. A belief system is the basis of group pride ... and the basis of group reward. What makes a good American? What makes a good Rotarian? What makes a good member of the Oakhurst

Elementary School PTA? You are a member in good standing when — and only when — you adhere to the fundamental belief system that the group has established. It is the basis of group sanction or group confrontation. If you do not have a belief system, how in the world can you criticize me if I behave as if I had none, either?

One of the things we have to get back to in America is peer confrontation. True peer confrontation does not exist until one party is willing to say to another: "I love you enough and you love me enough for me to tell you what is and is not acceptable." That was a mistake I made as a dad: assuming, because my children watched what we did in our family, they knew what we thought about things. It does not work that way. Today, we have to sit down and teach our children verbally. We have to spell it out: "Here is what we believe in this family, and this is why we believe it." And, doing just that is seldom an easy job.

What Should I Expect?

First, I suggest the basic fundamental of your belief system ought to at least cover what is a valid personal relationship? I am not going to tell you what that ought to be because it is vitally important that you decide what a valid personal relationship should be. You decide because you are the one who has to mirror that behavior. What is a valid personal relationship? You have to decide. You are the one who draws the line in the sand.

Second, what is your family's chemical use policy? You decide. At a minimum, it should be legal.

Third, what is your family's policy on expressing frustration, fear, or anger through physical force? Is it cowardly to run from a fight ... or the prudent thing to do? This can be a tough policy to clearly define.

And fourth, what is valid entertainment for members of this family? You decide what your family will and will not recognize as fun. If we choose to allow death to be recognized as fun, then we again must be willing to pay the price. Your family belief system can only be taught by you. No one else can teach it — no one else should teach it. That is your job; you must set the expectations… and you must enforce it!

What's In A Name ?

One way in which we often set expectations is through names and nicknames. The baby boy with Junior or III at the end of his name grows up with the expectation he will be a chip off the old block.

His or her name is very important to a child. It is the core of personal identity, the starting point of individual destiny and, in some cases, a link with the past. A popular trend within the African-American culture is to create names that are either a reflection of heritage or that are totally unique. In the Jewish culture, it is traditional to give a child the name of a relative of the same sex who has recently died. In the American South, it is a common practice to give a child a family sir name as a first name. Every distinct culture has its guidelines for the selection of names. The Roman Catholic Church believes so strongly in the power of names that its members who enter a religious order are given new names to signify a new beginning to their lives.

There is debate on the genesis of this Catholic tradition; however, it is an action that may come from the Bible. Jesus selected, as one of his disciples, a man named Simon. That name carried the meaning "indecisive" or, to be blunt, "wishy-washy." Simon was renamed Peter, which means "The Rock." And, the Bible tells of Simon Peter's struggle to live up to his new name and his triumph in doing just that.

While many cultures track the meaning of names, most of us have abandoned the practice. By not doing so, we are losing an opportunity to strengthen the bond between ourselves and our children. If you have given your child a name that has a family tie, let the child know the significance. If you have followed a growing movement in the African-American culture of giving your child a name that springs from your heritage or a unique name that no one else is likely to have, impress on the child the significance of having a unique name. And, if the name does not have a clear meaning, establish one by thinking through your reasons for creating or selecting that particular name.

Most established names have a meaning, and in any library or bookstore, you should find a book that defines names. Look up the meaning of your child's name and, while you are at it, look up the meaning of yours. When I tried this, I learned that my name, William, means "resolute protector." I like that. My wife's name is Vicky, which means "overcomer or victorious spirit." The name of my daughter who got into The Toxic Culture is Peggy, which means "gift of God." And the name of my other daughter is Julie, "seeker of truth." So, when we have our little family meetings, no matter how jerky we may all have been, there is Resolute Protector, Victorious Spirit, Gift of God, and Seeker of Truth present.

Look at my Grandkids:

Penelope is of Greek origin, and the meaning of Penelope is "weaver". From "pene". Mythology: Penelope, wife of Odysseus, fended off suitors by weaving during the day and unraveling at night a tapestry she said had to be completed before she would wed another husband. The name has come to signify a loyal, capable, and clever woman.

Louis as a boy's name is pronounced LOO-iss, loo-WEE. It is of French and Old German origin, and the meaning of Louis is "famous warrior".

Emily as a girl's name is pronounced EM-i-ee. It is of Latin origin, and the meaning of Emily is "rival; laborious; eager". From the Latin name Aemilia, feminine form of the old Roman surname Aemilius.

Cate as a girl's name is a variant of Catherine (Greek), Kate and Katherine (Greek), and the meaning of Cate is "pure".

Will means "desiring peace; as with a helmet, protector".

Luke \l(u)-ke\ as a boy's name is pronounced look. It is of Greek origin, and the meaning of Luke is "from Lucanus". Place name: a region in southern Italy. Also sometimes used as an English form of Lucius and Lucian. Biblical: a first-century Christian, called "the beloved physician" and is patron saint of doctors and artists, who wrote one of the four Gospel accounts of the life of Christ.

Maybe it's just me, but these are amazingly accurate.

Give your child a positive nickname

Here is another technique, one I learned from my daughter Julie.

Nicknames are also important. They are a tool that helps the child look within to identify their character, their special strengths, and uniqueness. When my youngest daughter, Julie, was little, she was, frankly, the ugliest kid you ever saw. Dynamically ugly: big, thick Coke-bottle glasses, pigtails, buck teeth with braces, Kool-Aid stain on her lip. When she was about eleven, one day she said to me, "Dad, you know what? I'm going to be beautiful when I grow up."

I wish you could see her today. She is absolutely gorgeous. You know what she nicknamed herself? She started calling herself Jewels. To this day, we receive phone calls and letters from our Jewels.

Few of us, however, nickname ourselves. And, so often we give children negative nicknames. Give your child a positive one. Find a character trait at which the child excels or one you want to encourage and nickname them that. They will love it. It is intimacy. It is recognition. It is Maslow's atomic bomb wrapped up in a moniker. Gangs know the power of nicknames. The first thing a gang gives a kid is a nickname. Nicknames create a sense of both belonging and individual identity. Let's not allow gangs to have a monopoly on such an important parenting tool.

Some nicknames become goals to be obtained. For example, when Oral Hersheiser first went to the Dodgers, he was not an aggressive pitcher. Tommy Lasorda, the Dodgers' manager at the time, decided that no one named Oral Hersheiser could be aggressive; so, he started calling Hersheiser "The Bulldog." That changed Hersheiser's approach to pitching. He became a bulldog because of his new mental picture of himself. We all tend to live up to ... or down to ... others' image of ourselves. The power of nicknames to establish a positive or negative image should not be ignored.

Traditions and Family History

Neither should we ignore the power of sharing family traditions. Traditions are another means of setting expectations and creating commitment to the family belief system. The perpetuation of family traditions was second nature to previous generations. A few decades ago, we still learned family history because we lived with it. As families move farther and farther apart, we now need to consciously perpetuate traditions that are in danger of fading away. We also should create new ones because family traditions give a child both a sense of uniqueness and a sense of belonging. They cause a child to look within for personal strengths and abilities. So, consciously talk about the past. Consciously swap stories. Consciously spell out the significance of that fading snap shot, that frayed old quilt, that scar on your arm.

Sharing history and tradition is a means of bonding the child with the family belief system and setting expectations that highlight the importance of character. Share your family history with your children. I do not mean drag out the genealogy charts; however, that may prove interesting to some youngsters. The stories you pass along do not all have to deal with heroic acts or herculean accomplishments. I am talking about sharing your history: your childhood memories, your dating experiences, even the occasions in your life when you blew it socially. At a time when one of my girls was feeling particularly uncool, telling the following story made a difference.

My wife, Vicky, and I had our first date when I was fifteen. We went to a movie in a big movie theater, and I had bragged to my buddies that I had a date with the most beautiful girl they had ever seen. After the movie, we left our seats in the balcony and started descending the giant staircase into the lobby, where my friends were waiting to check out my date. Vicky tripped and tumbled halfway down the steps. I picked her up and asked if she was okay. "Yeah, I'm fine. Please let me go." I did, and she rolled the rest of the way down the grand staircase. My kids love that story because it makes us parents human.

Did you make straight A's in every course you ever took? Probably not, but your children think you did. One of the happiest days in my daughter's life, was finding her mother's report card.

Keep Old Family Traditions And Create New Ones.

Traditions build desirable expectations within you and within your child. Traditions set standards for the child to live up to and expectations from the child of meaningful interaction and support from the family. If you do not have them, start them. If you have a few, create more. Traditions make the family unique, different, and special. One of ours started with an orange tree that grew in our yard, when we lived in Florida. Our first orange crop was one orange. A single orange. At Christmas, Vicky's parents were there, and I joked about celebrating the Oliver Family Orange Festival. The idea grew into plans for a ceremony that included picking and slicing the orange into slices for one and all. Vicky's father was selected for the honor, and we captured the moment on video tape. The orange was picked, transported into the house on a silver platter, and sliced. As he handed each person a portion, he said, "This means good health next year." This became a holiday tradition that our girls cherish to this day.

Think back to your childhood and what was really important to you. I suggest that many of your fondest memories and the moments that strengthened family bonds were those involving traditions that celebrated character, charm and charisma. That special food prepared to celebrate an accomplishment or a special occasion. That trunk of old clothes your grandmother kept for you to play "dress up." The crazy uncle who used to perform card tricks, when you went to visit him. You likely have traditions that you do not recognize as such because they are not connected to a holiday or special event, such as graduations or weddings. But, to the child who looks forward to the tradition — even if it is as simple as the nightly reading of a bedtime story or being tucked in with a kiss for the kid and another for his favorite teddy bear — it is an honored tradition, one filled with ceremony and ritual.

For example, when the grandchildren of a friend of mine come to visit, she makes certain that the golf cart's battery has a good charge on it because her grandchildren look forward to riding in it with her ... and eventually becoming old enough to scoot around her spacious yard in it by themselves. To them, this is a grand tradition, one associated only with visits to Grandmother's house. To the son of a friend of mine, it is the ritual of helping his dad tidy up the tackle box and make certain all the fishing gear he and his dad will use on their next outing is in ship-shape.

Reading to children is a tradition every parent should perpetuate. A variation on reading the classic children's stories is telling them with a personal twist. For example, when I tell my four-year-old grandson, whose name is William Irvin, the tale of Jack and the Beanstalk, it becomes the tale of Sir William of Irvin and the Beanstalk. When I tell my granddaughter Emily time-honored stories, they are about Lady Emily's adventures, many of which are the same stories I tell my grandson. Customizing classics bolsters children's imaginations and sense of personal uniqueness. It is just one of hundreds of ways we can celebrate the average child.

How Should I Inspect?

We have spent a great deal of time setting our personal expectations of our child and learning how to help the child set expectations of himself or herself. Now, it is time to explore how we should inspect to see if we are getting what we expect. The two words are companions. One needs the other.

There is an old saying among farmers that the quality of the crop is in direct proportion to the number of a farmer's footprints in his field. Inspecting is the way we show love for the crop. It is not snooping. It is not being a busy body. It is the way we show love. When I come home from a trip, one of the first things I do is inspect my wife. I want to know if she is smiling. I want to know if she is frustrated. I want to know if she is happy. I want to know if she is sad. What is her mental and emotional state? If I simply walked into the house, say "How are you?" and turned on the television set, what would I be telling my wife? I would be telling her, "You're not important to me." However, since she is extremely important to me, I inspect.

When we inspect our children, we are looking to see their character. We are looking for their personal uniqueness. We are looking for their strengths. We are looking for what is right about them — not just the areas where they need our help to improve.

As parents, we back away from inspection of our teenagers because we are afraid they will think we are nosy. They may even tell you that you are being nosy, but that is not what they feel. What they feel is not very different from when they were little and came home to the question: "How was school today?" In response, they proudly showed you a drawing the teacher had awarded a star or a paper on which the teacher had marked an A. When they presented that trophy of accomplishment, you placed it on the refrigerator door so that everyone could admire it. For some reason when children get older, we become afraid to inspect, even though we know that inspection is the way we show love.

The opposite of inspection is ignoring a person, and the message we broadcast loud and clear by that action is "You don't matter." You may have the nastiest, ugliest, dirtiest, meanest kid in the world and tell me that when you inspect him or her you see nothing good. You certainly, want to inspect them to look for the good. So often we parents, as mentioned earlier, interact with our kids by primarily criticizing them. "Your room's dirty ... Bet you haven't finished your homework ... Why don't you do something about your hair?" Suppose I walked into my house and greeted my wife with "The den's dirty ... Did you get the bills paid?" How long do you think that would last? Not very long with my wife. There is good in everyone, at least a spark of it. It is up to us to kindle that spark in our children. Positive inspection says, "I love you and am looking for behavior I can praise."

So, while you should not overlook or ignore your child's shortcomings, you should look within him or her for reasons to celebrate. Yes, celebrate the average child. Do not forget that average children make up the majority of us. Remember the power of the ordinary person and do not devalue it. In fact, I suggest that you look closely at your children until you find they are doing something flat average. Then, have a victory celebration. When you do, they will raise their confidence and their standard about a foot. Celebrate that next level of accomplishment, and they will raise the standard another foot.

Positive expectation and inspection not only can be a lot of fun, in tandem they are the real basis for intimacy in your family

CHAPTER SEVEN

NEVER GIVE IN

"Never give in—never, never, never, never, in nothing great or small, large or petty, never give in except to convictions of honor and good sense. Never yield to force; never yield to the apparently overwhelming might of the enemy."

Sir Winston Churchill, *Speech, 1941, Harrow School*

The N in our acrostic stands for Never Give In.

In 1941, Britain was being pummeled By The Nazis. London was being bombed. Supply lines from America had been all but severed by German Wolf-packs. Things not only looked bleak... They were bleak.

Harrow School was a prestigious, private school for boys and Winston Churchill had been asked to give a speech to encourage the British People. He closed his speech with the above words, "Never Give In. Never... Never... Never."

Not bad advice for Parents. Never Give In... Never!

Realize this. The Toxic Culture will never go away. It has been around since the days of Ancient Rome and even before that. Evil will always be among us and you will not change that. But, you do not have to surrender your children and your family to it.

It starts with a zero tolerance of illicit drug use in your family, violent entertainment in your home, and premature sex by your children.

The Camel In The Tent!

One of my favorite illustrations has to do with an Arab Bedouin who was approached by his camel asking to sleep in the tent one night because it was tired of being cold. Obviously, the Bedouin refused to allow that. The camel then suggested a compromise. "Then at least let me put my nose under the tent flap so that I can breathe the warm air." the camel said. The Bedouin, being a kind- hearted man, allowed that. The next morning when the Arab awoke, the camel was fully in the tent... along with his wife and two children.

I submit that letting the Toxic Culture's nose into your tent is a BIG Mistake. It is the beginning of "Giving In".

The Tent And The Car

There are two places that you definitely can control... your home (tent) and your car. Here are some options you might consider.

Enforce the Game and Movie Rating Systems: These rating systems are actually good in and of themselves. The problem is that they are not generally enforced. Most of us don't even know what they mean.

Here are those Categories for Games:

Ce

EARLY CHILDHOOD:

Content is intended for young children.

E

EVERYONE Content is generally suitable for all ages. May contain minimal cartoon, fantasy or mild violence and/or infrequent use of mild language.

E10+

EVERYONE 10+ Content is generally suitable for ages 10 and up. May contain more cartoon, fantasy or mild violence, mild language and/or minimal suggestive themes.

T

TEEN is generally suitable for ages 13 and up. May contain violence, suggestive themes, crude humor, minimal blood, simulated gambling and/or infrequent use of strong language.

M

MATURE Content is generally suitable for ages 17 and up. May contain intense violence, blood and gore, sexual content and/or strong language.

A

ADULTS ONLY Content suitable only for adults ages 18 and up. May include prolonged scenes of intense violence, graphic sexual content and/or gambling with real currency.

PR

> Rating Pending Not yet assigned a final ESRB rating. Appears only in advertising, marketing and promotional materials related to a game that is expected to carry an ESRB rating, and should be replaced by a game's rating once it has been assigned.

Don't those make sense? All you have to do is follow the Entertainment Industry Recommendations. Ignore them at your own peril!!! Movies have a similar system.

The Toxic Culture Is Using Technology...

Recommendation: Don't Fight It! Use It! Let it help you do your job.

Here are some things to consider:

Net Nanny: I am a big fan of a service called Net Nanny. It let's you set all kinds of limits on Internet usage. Among its many features it lets YOU:

> Block pornography from appearing on your computer.
>
> Mask profanity before it appears on the screen.
>
> Monitor social media to find out who your kids are talking to.
>
> Control access to set time limits on Internet usage.
>
> Monitor Instant Message (IM) to identify potential predators and protect against cyber-bullying.
>
> Send alerts and reports to your console or email.
>
> Control video games to only allow the games you want to be played.

Create user profiles to tailor protection to your individual family members' needs.

And just how much does this cost? **$59.98 A Year** to protect three computers. At that price, it is a MUST HAVE in every home.

Visit **http://www.netnanny.com** to see more.

Smart Phones: Every child should have one. Used properly, they are like an electronic leash on your child. I don't know about all of them, but the Apple iPhone has a wonderful little App called Find My iPhone. It uses GPS to locate the IPhone and plot it on a map.

That's right... plot its location on a map. Insist that your child have that iPhone with them at all times. Tell them that you may call that number at any time and they have four rings to answer it. If it is not answered promptly, you will launch the FBI... Family Bureau Of Investigation and conduct an investigation as to their location. You will then proceed to that location for an "On-site" visit.

Another benefit of the Smart Phone is that the bill from Verizon, ATT, et al, will show the phone's call record for the month:

Who called whom.

Time of call.

Length of call.

Frequency of call.

The Phone Number of the third party.

That is better than a Private Detective.

GPS Car Tracking: There are "relatively" cheap Tracking Devices ($200+ and $25/Month) that will automatically track your car. For example: The cars location and routes, by detailed color map, satellite image and address;

Online Reports of Mileage, Stops and Moves;

The details of the continuous activity for any time during the past 6 months;

Any instances that the vehicle has been speeding (you set the limits);

Any instances that the vehicle enters or exits any of up to 3 of your preset boundaries;

Instant alerts to any number of cellphones and/or emails when any speeding or boundary violation occurs;

24/7 Support from Customer Service Center.

Cost: About $19.95 per month after an initial investment of about $250 for the device. One I have heard about is **http://gpsteentracking.com**. Check it out!!!

Drug Testing Services: Too intrusive? Maybe. Maybe not. I think not.

Sooner or later your child will be Drug Tested by Home Depot, Delta Airlines, Motorola, Texas Instruments, The NFL and a host of well run companies… not to mention the US Military.

Why do companies do that? Are they just nosey?

The answer is no. The fact is that the drug-using employee is too expensive to have on the Payroll. Their accident rates are higher than the non-user. Their Absentee rates are higher than the non-user. On top of that, they are less productive than their non-using coworker.

Companies have found that sensible drug testing is also a terrific Prevention Program. "I would love to party with you guys but my company might test me…" a great reason to Just Say No!

The **PDT 90** is one tool to consider. It is deadly accurate and reasonably priced. The company says this:

"The Psychemedics® PDT-90 Hair Test is the first internationally patented test technology for drug abuse analysis. It offers you a personal drug history over a 90 day period and detects Marijuana, Ecstasy (MDMA), Cocaine (including crack), Opiates (including heroin), Methamphetamine, and Phencyclidine (PCP or angel dust)."

The confidential PDT-90 hair drug test analysis has consistently proven to be more effective than urinalysis and other methods in correctly identifying substance abusers. In fact, when hair vs. urine results were compared in "side-by-side" evaluation, 5 to 10 times as many drug abusers were accurately identified with the PDT-90 kit.

The PDT 90 Test Kit is available in many chain Drugstores, Walgreens, etc. Talk to your local Pharmacist.

See their website:

http://www.psychemedics.com

The Smell Test: No kit needed. Just your nose. Just sniff around your child's room, clothes, and friends. If something smells funny, it probably is.

But Wait There's More…

Allow me to introduce The Toxic Culture's worst nightmare.

Please meet:

MammaRuski

My niece, a Washington D.C Attorney and mother of two, on occasion, becomes the all powerful, all knowing MammaRuski.

Her kids, both of whom are now finishing college, told me about Nancy's transformation into MammaRuski as the occasion demanded. Nancy is a terrific Christian Lady... mild mannered... even tempered... a gentle and deeply caring soul. Her kids report that his was her normal temperament.

If, however, Nancy became aware that something might be amiss with her kids, she became the creature from Hell (their words), MammaRuski. MammaRuski would not rest until the she was satisfied that there were no camels in her tent... around her tent, ... or close to her tent... whatever it took. Once the "evil was exorcised", she reverted to the mild mannered, saintly Mother Nancy, but until then...

MammaRuski is the greatest drug prevention, sex prevention, and violence prevention program ever developed.

Very few girls have gotten pregnant, very few teens have gotten high, and very few episodes of violence have occurred with "MammaRuski" lurking nearby.

MammaRuski lives by the Old Russian proverb, "Trust But Verify."

One other thing to note. MammaRuski is completely intolerant of Toxic Activities by her kids. She knows that old Management Principle: "To Tolerate A Behavior Is To Teach That Very Behavior. "

Her kids knew that MammaRuski would Never Give In... Never... Never... Never...

So they did!

The MammaRuski Principle

"If MammaRuski Ain't Happy, Ain't Nobody Happy!"

CHAPTER EIGHT

TRAPS TO AVOID

The last letter in our acrostic, P.A.R.E.N.T., is T. It stands for Traps to Avoid. As I was developing my list of traps, I realized that the first three on my list closely duplicated what the great Civil Rights leader and peace mediator Mahatma Gandhi said were among the deadly sins that nations must avoid. When he made his list, back in the 1940's, he added: nations that fall into these traps are doomed to fail. Let's examine three of Gandhi's warnings from a parenting point of view.

Wealth Without Work, Education Without Character, and Entertainment Without Conscience.

Dr. Gandhi headed his list of sins with **Wealth Without Work**, a warning to the world's most affluent nations. We have not heeded his warning. In fact, in highly affluent America, it is our children who are the ones most likely to be taught and believe that Wealth Without Work is a worthy goal. For example, if you watch television at all, you have at least stumbled on the thirty minute pitches called "infomercials." Some sell products that are supposed to radically change your life with little or no effort on your part. Others sell get-rich-quick schemes of various sorts. All you have to do, so they say, is buy their course and you will become an instant millionaire. You do not even have to show up for work. Just place a few ads in the newspaper and you are on your way to living in the lap of luxury. In one guise or another, the idea of Wealth Without Work is sold all the time to us in our

American culture. Win the lottery. Become a movie star over night and get$ 20 million a film. Day trade your way to riches.

Gandhi's concern over wealth without work easily translates into benefit without effort, an idea that has been firmly planted in our children's minds. Furthermore, we love our children so much we knock ourselves out minimizing effort from their lives. For instance, we become so concerned with the child making an A or B that, instead of letting them struggle and exert the necessary effort to make a high grade, we do the project for them. That is benefit without effort, wealth without work.

I suggest that any time your children want or need anything, let them earn it. I have a neighbor who does a noteworthy job of raising kids. For example, every summer I can count on his son Chris knocking on my door in search of work that will earn his spending money for the family's annual vacation trip. Every summer, little Chris shows up, asking if I have any work for him. Each year, I say the same thing: "Well, Chris, I need the sticks picked up in my yard."

Since I literally live in the woods, I really do not care whether the sticks are picked up or not, but I want to do my part toward helping Chris learn that work is valuable. When he comes to the door and announces he is finished, I go with him for a tour to admire his handiwork, then pay him. What he earns is more than the dollars I shell out; what he earns is the value or accomplishment.

So, let me suggest that the next time you spot some kids operating a lemonade stand, stop and buy some of that lemonade. You don't have to drink it, but do buy it because those are young people who are trying to earn their way and are keeping alive the work ethic on which this country was built.

Gandhi was right; we will lose this country if we fail to teach our kids the benefit of work. The idea of wealth without work firmly plants in their heads the idea that the activity must be enjoyable. So, the toxic kid asks: "Is the activity fun, regardless of the result?" while the healthy kid asks: "Is the result beneficial to me?"

Education Without Character

The second deadly sin that Gandhi identified was Education Without Character. We have become so concerned about high school and college transcripts we forget something that Dr. Martin Luther King, Jr. pointed out: the content of a child's transcript is not as important as the content of the child's character.

Of course education is important. And transcripts are very meaningful to you while you are in the educational environment. However, once you land your first job, that transcript becomes virtually meaningless. When was the last time anyone asked to see your high school or college transcript? At job interviews, what they want to know is what you accomplished on your last job. That matters. Closer to home, your new neighbors are not interested in whether or not you made the dean's list; they want to know what type of neighbor you are, what you did, are doing, and plan to do to make your neighborhood a better one.

Some of the most successful and worthwhile people I can name did not have the luxury of completing high school. However, I know an awful lot of failures with all A's on their transcript. Our challenge in American today is not to raise smarter kids; it is to raise better ADULTS, ADULTS with character. One dictionary definition of the word "character" is to stamp, to imprint, or to engrave. That tells us that character is not something that simply happens. It is something imprinted on a person by others. As parents, it is our job to do the imprinting and do it so well that doing the right thing becomes our child's reflex reaction. In other words, character is what one does when no one is looking.

I seriously doubt that any drug dealers are reading this book, but I can assure you that most of you readers could make more money dealing drugs than you are making doing what you do. So, why aren't you out selling drugs? You aren't because of something called character, something our parents taught us by word and by deed. Our parents worked. They were merchants, farmers, attorneys, teachers, salesmen, doctors, nurses, repairmen, and policemen. But few, if any of us, had a parent who was a movie star, a rock star, or a sports star. So, why are we holding such people up to our children as role models? Our children's chances of wearing a Super Bowl ring or of being given an Oscar are not as good as their chances of being hit by lightening or of winning the lottery. It is the job of our schools to teach our children English and algebra. But, the job of teaching character falls at our feet. It falls to us because we are primary in the lives of our children.

Entertainment Without Conscience

Gandhi's third warning, issued in the 1940's, was against Entertainment Without Conscience. This warning, along with his first two against Wealth Without Work and Education Without Conscience, sums up America today.

A number of years ago, there was a popular series of films called Faces of Death. I doubt that you have seen any of these films, but I can assure you that most fifth and sixth grade kids have. These documentaries rarely played in movie theaters; they were and still are distributed through neighborhood video stores. These are films that show no actors, have no special effects. Their content consists entirely of real people dying violently.

Does it shock you that Faces of Death was so popular there was sequel after sequel? If you own a TV set, it shouldn't. Today we have for prime time entertainment America's most violent real life police chases. We have street brawls masquerading as the sport of wrestling. We sit and watch both documented and fictionalized mayhem every night. We sit and we watch with our children and think absolutely nothing about it. Yet following a school massacre, we ponder what caused this kid to do this horrible thing.

Entertainment without Conscience is unworthy of our children. Beyond the obvious reasons, there is the fact that, in the minds of very young children, there is no difference between a real event and a picture of an event. We should not expect them to differentiate. After all, as adults we go to the movies and become lost in the story that is unfolding on the screen. We have to remind ourselves that it is only a movie. The monster stalking the terrified heroine is special effects; there is no real cause for fear. During other movies, we try to stop ourselves from tearing up; after all, before the movie ends, Robin Williams will surely be cured of cancer.

I am not saying there is anything wrong in your losing your grasp of reality and becoming involved in the story as it unfolds on the screen. You are an adult with the ability to sort out fact from fiction. You have the ability to check yourself and acknowledge that it is only a movie. But, can a six-year-old be expected to do the same? Can a six-year old be expected to differentiate between the mass murder shown on the six o'clock news and the mass murder shown in a prime time drama?

Even dearly loved films often contain elements that should not be imposed on small children. Bambi, for example. Go back and recall that G-rated classic. What do you remember about it?

When I ask this question in seminars, the invariable answer is when the hunters stalk down and kill Bambi's mother. For about an hour, you had bonded with Bambi and his family. You had grown to love them, care about them, and personally identify with Bambi. Then you were suddenly subjected to the death of his mother — in your mind the death of your own mother, the experience of abandonment. You cried. Perhaps you were one of the scores of children who had to be taken outside, at that point.

Yes, death is a fact of life. Yes, cruelty is a fact of life. But do our children need to be immersed in death, in cruelty, and in violence before they are old enough to tie their shoe laces? Do we need to feed our children a steady prime time diet of television violence and promiscuous sex in order to prep them for the real world? Do we really need "games like Doom and Grand Theft Auto in our homes?

The recent criticism of the entertainment industry's obsession with violence has brought about a slight reduction in the amount of it on television. But, the violence has not been replaced with a contemporary Mayberry or the foibles of Winnie the Poo. No, it has been replaced with sex, which the entertainment industry knows sells just as well as blood and guts. Our children are continuing to be served up entertainment without conscience. Therefore, we should not be surprised when our children emulate the amoral behavior they see.

I am not saying that all television is bad. There is at least an hour's worth of daily programming that is appropriate for young minds. And that is about as much television as any child needs.

Adulthood Without Childhood

For the remaining four traps for parents to avoid, we move from Gandhi's list to Oliver's list. Each trap is one I have learned about the hard way. One of them is the idea of Adulthood without Childhood. We are rushing our children. From the day we bring them home from the hospital, we start dressing them like tiny adults. The fact of the matter is somewhere around the fifth or sixth grade, our little girls start to look like little twenty-five year olds and our little boys start to look like thirty-something. So, it shouldn't surprise us when they start trying to play "adult games" that adults do not play.

Let me give you an example of what I mean when I say Adulthood without Childhood. How would you feel if my wife and I called you to say, "We're going to get together with five or six other couples over at our house this Saturday night for a co-ed spend the night party. Would you and your spouse or you and your boyfriend or girlfriend bring your pajamas for a co-ed spend-the-night party in our basement?"

If I did, you would think I had lost my mind. You would think it because that is a game most adults do not play. But that is a game children in your community play time and time again. You might respond, "But the church has lock-ins, right?" Well, I am for your children and mine going to a lock-in where there is a minister awake and on duty full-time and there am a lot of praying and scripture reading taking place. But that is not what is happening at neighborhood co-ed pajama parties, now is it? And we had better admit to that fact.

Another mimicry of adulthood is spring break, that springtime ritual of going to the beach with a dozen or so buddies for a three-day drunk. While that is a game rational, sane adults do not play, it is a game we allow children to play. It is accepted. It is even financed by parents. Situations, such as these two examples from a long, long list I could place before you, prove that one of the things you, as a parent, in today's Toxic Culture, have to fight for the hardest is the childhood of your child. You have to fight because today's Toxic Culture wants to rush your child into a sick caricature of supposed adulthood. There is no reason to rush; your child will be an adult for a long, long time. Let them be children, a least for a few years.

Freedom Without Accountability

The fifth of the seven parent traps to avoid is Freedom without Accountability. Earlier, I noted freedom is always earned, and trust is always earned — never given. That means there is another trap out there, waiting for us. We parents want to give our kids the idea that we trust them; so, we stop holding them accountable for what they are doing. When we do, we do not fulfill one of our obligations as parents. I firmly believe that we have an obligation, on evenings when our teenagers have been out, to wait up for them and ask, "Where have you been? What have you done? Whom were you with? And what happened?"

Here is the problem. We were once children, too, and we did some things that were simply stupid. We did some things that we are not exactly proud of. I know I am not the only one because at every seminar I hold, some parent says: "Well, Bill, I did this or that when I was a kid. Isn't it hypocritical for me to hold my child accountable?"

The psychobabblists say our generation of parents is "conflicted". I suggest you get "unconflicted" as soon as possible. So, you did a lot of stupid things. But you do not want your children repeating the same mistakes — much less making worse ones. If we are not going to teach our children the results of what we learned, we may as well not be in the house. You rode your bicycle without a helmet, didn't you? You drove in a car without a seat belt, didn't you? But does that mean you shouldn't tell you children to wear a helmet and a seat belt? Of course not. You should hold them accountable for doing these things because they are the wise, the safe, and the sensible things to do. The same holds true with any of the toxic dangers on which we are focusing in this book. They need to know your position on each and every subject.

At seminars, I also hear parents ask, "Suppose my child asks me if I did these things, should I tell them?" If you ask the experts that question, you are going to get a range of answers. One expert is going to say, "Yes, you tell them because you don't want them finding out later that you held something back." And another range of experts is going to say, "No, you don't tell them that because you don't confess your sins to a thirteen-year-old." Now, I'm going to suggest a middle ground that covers both of those extremes. When asked, do not say "yes", do not say "no". Let this be your answer: "Darling, I did a lot of things when I was a kid that you're not going to do. Which stupid things I did or did not do has no bearing on what you're allowed to do. I've learned a lot, and I can assure you in this family no one is going to do that."

Why do I say to answer it that way? Here's why. If your answer is "Yes, I did that," your child's immediate mental response will be: "So, I can do that. You did it, and got away with it. Look at you. You did drugs and you did all this stuff. You were a wild party man, and look at you now. You're a lawyer, you're a preacher, you're a doctor." In other words, a "yes" becomes implied permission to go and do likewise.

If you answer the same question, "No, I didn't do that," the child will interpret your answer to mean that you have no practical experience with the matter and simply do not know what you are talking about.

Either way you become a dead duck, if you give a straightforward affirmative or negative answer. However, saying that you did a lot of stupid things that you will not tolerate in your family is an honest answer that sets limits and expectations.

The real question they are asking is not "Did you do that?"; the real question is "May I do that?" So, get right to the point; say: "The real question you're asking is can you get away with doing that. And, the answer is 'No you cannot.' Any stupid things I did while growing up are not the issue here. The limits concerning what you may and may not do are set in concrete.

That answers the real question … the question behind the question.

Love Without Limits

The next trap that parents fall into also concerns limits and expectations. It is the trap of Love without Limits. I will not belabor the point. Love always sets limits. It is by setting limits that we have freedom. It is by setting limits that we have family. It is by setting limits that we know we are loved. Supposed I come home from a business trip and tell my wife I have been painting the town with some woman I met at my hotel. And, suppose her reaction is "No big deal." What would that tell me? It would tell me she does not care, does not love me.

The way we know someone loves us is by the limits they set. They set limits to protect us, to keep us safe. Limits are one part of the language of love. That is how we must show our children love: through limits. We tell them we are not going to let them kill themselves. We must tell them we love them enough to forbid them to get into a position where they can be swept away by the Toxic Culture. We tell them we love them so much we will plant ourselves in the doorway and stand between them and danger. We tell them we know what others do, but our children will not participate. That is a clear expression of love.

I am going to tell you about something of which I am not proud. When we were having trouble with our daughter, I taped her phone conversations. I went to Radio Shack and bought a device that enabled me to hear conversations that included: "Oh, don't worry about my Daddy. He's a sucker." That is what my daughter thought of me. She thought it because I was a sucker. I had set no limits on her life whatsoever. And having no limits almost killed her. Limits are love. Set them. And enforce them.

Life Without a Vision

The final trap I point out is probably the most dangerous of all: Life without a Vision. Research clearly reveals children who have a vision of the future do far better than children who do not have a vision of the future. Some years ago, I read a book that made me realize how critical having a vision of the future is. The book, Man's Search for Meaning, is by Victor Frankl, an Austrian psychiatrist in 1930's. When Hitler came into power in Austria and Germany, Frankl was thrown into a concentration camp because he was a Jew. In that camp, he was separated from his wife, separated from his children. He was stripped of everything he had. His clothes were taken from him, his name was taken from him, the hair on his body was shaved, the manuscript he had spent his life writing was trampled into the dirt of a latrine. In a matter of hours he had gone from a fairly sane world to one of utter horror.

Because he was a psychiatrist and a student of mankind, he started asking himself why is it that some people are surviving this insane environment? Why have some survived years of starvation, cold, and slave labor, while others who were physically stronger died in a matter of weeks? He concluded, that the survivors were the ones who dreamed about a day when they would go back home. They projected a vision of the future that made even life in a concentration camp worth living. In a word, they had hope.

All of us can survive horrible, insane times as long as we have a clear vision of the future that is grounded in hope. Therefore, one of the things that disturbs me about our kids today is I am afraid we are not teaching them to dream, to project a vision, to fill their hearts with hope. Our children are being told by national leaders that they will be the first generation of Americans to live worse than their parents. When I hear that, I want to stand up and shout, "Only if they believe it!"

If you truly want your child's life to be better than yours, I have a recommendation for you. Tonight, sit down with your child and ask him or her the question you were probably asked by every significant adult in your life, that question you were asked from age three on: "What are you going to be when you grow up?" That is a question I have not heard asked a child in years. I am not certain I ever asked either of my children what they wanted to be when they grew up.

It is an important question. It is a question that lets your child know three important things. Firstly, it lets the child know he or she will grow up. It says neither childhood nor adolescence are permanent conditions. Secondly, it says to your child that he or she is going to be something. Even the choice to be nothing is a choice to be something. Thirdly, the question tells your child he or she will have to make a choice. Yes, asking, "What are you going to be when you grow up?" is a very powerful question.

When I make this suggestion, I am frequently asked, "But what about the little child who doesn't have a vision, doesn't have a dream?" My response is always the same: that is the very kid who must be asked the question. That is the very kid, of all of them, whom we want to realize he or she is going to be something and does have a choice.

I suggest to you that the family's role, that your role as a father, your role as a mother, is to discover the dream that was built into each kid the day he or she was born. I am convinced in my heart that every kid born has some talent, some gift, some ability that is unique on the face of the earth. And like mining for a diamond, it is our job as parents to discover the gift. I recommend you have your child tested.

The tests may predict a business person, a salesperson, a caterer, or any number of other honorable professions. Remember that this country was built and continues being built and run today by ordinary people who do extraordinary things in their lives.

I assure you that all the ordinary people who accomplished something extraordinary had one thing in common: all, somewhere along the way, met an adult who viewed them as individuals with unique talents and abilities. Find your child's unique talents and abilities, build a curriculum, if you will, in your family that mines and refines. Life without a vision, life without a dream is merely existence without hope.

I read a suicide note by a young man of sixteen. His mother brought it to me at the end of one of my classes, one in which we had been talking about the sex, the drugs, and the violence of the Toxic Culture. She said, "I want you to read this. I want you to read my son's suicide note."

I accepted the piece of paper, unfolded it, and saw these words: "I tried it all. I've done it all. I think I'll try this. Mom, I love you."

That is a chilling summation of the effects of America's Toxic Culture on one family. And, you are the primary person responsible for protecting your child from it.

You can do this!

You Must Do This!

Along the way, you will meet three friends, a Scarecrow, a Tin Woodsman, and a Lion... Wisdom, Love, and Courage. They will see you home!

What's Next?

Create A Parent Circle

Form a peer group of like minded parents consisting of the Moms and Dads of your childs "BFF's". Probably not more than five or so families. Keep it small.

Share this book with them.

After they have read it, hold a MammaRuski discussion "party" to set group standards regarding:

> Off Limits Times
> Off Limits Places
> Off Limits People
> Off Limits Activities
> Off Limits Substances
> Consequences For Violations

Network With Each Other
> Facebook
> Twitter
> Text
> Telephone

Trust But Verify... And Verify... And Verify... And Verify!

STAY IN TOUCH

As I mentioned earlier, use technology to help you raise your kids in today's world. Passage Group Publishing has a Facebook Page so that we, the parents, can stay in touch. You can also use this, to network with other parents sharing your goal and vision... and challenges. The kids are networked... why not us?

Visit And "Like" Us At:

www.facebook.com/PassagePublishing.

Recommended Reading

Gifts Differing by Isabel and Peter Myers

Co-Dependent No More by Melody Beattie

Stop Teaching Our Kids To Kill by Dave Grossman

Raising Teens Isn't Easy by Operation Parent

The Wizard Of Oz by L. Frank Baum

CPSIA information can be obtained at www.ICGtesting.com
Printed in the USA
BVOW081859300413
319521BV00003B/204/P